Geometry

**LARSON
BOSWELL
STIFF**

Applying • Reasoning • Measuring

Standardized Test Practice Workbook

The Standardized Test Practice Workbook provides practice exercises for every lesson in a standardized test format. Included are multiple-choice, quantitative-comparison, and multi-step problems.

McDougal Littell
A HOUGHTON MIFFLIN COMPANY

Evanston, Illinois • Boston • Dallas

ISBN-13: 978-0-618-02086-7   ISBN-10: 0-618-02086-1

15 16 17 18 19 20 - DOM - 11 10 09 08

Contents

Standardized Test Practice

For use with pages 3–9

TEST TAKING STRATEGY   **Read each test question carefully. Always look for short-cuts that will allow you to work through a problem more quickly.**

1. *Multiple Choice* Choose the next figure in the pattern.

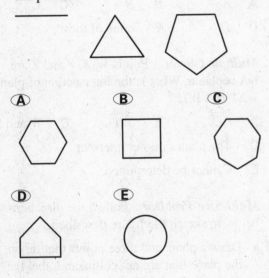

2. *Multiple Choice* What is the next number in the sequence?

2, −1, −4, −7 . . .

Ⓐ −9   Ⓑ −10   Ⓒ 10

Ⓓ −11   Ⓔ −12

3. *Multiple Choice* What is the next number in the sequence?

0, 2, 6, 12 . . .

Ⓐ 18   Ⓑ 24   Ⓒ 20

Ⓓ 22   Ⓔ 26

4. *Multiple Choice* What is the next number in the sequence?

−2, 4, 16 . . .

Ⓐ 28   Ⓑ 26   Ⓒ −12

Ⓓ 256   Ⓔ 192

5. *Multiple Choice* Choose the next figure in the pattern.

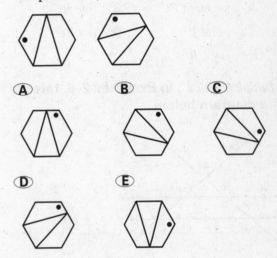

6. *Multiple Choice* The first three objects in a pattern are shown. How many blocks are in the next object?

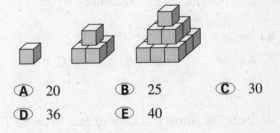

Ⓐ 20   Ⓑ 25   Ⓒ 30

Ⓓ 36   Ⓔ 40

7. *Multi-Step Problem* Examine the triangular pattern.

```
        1
      1   1
    1   2   1
  1   3   3   1
```

a. Predict the next two rows of the triangle.

b. Describe a pattern for the value of a number in each row.

c. Describe a pattern for the number of entries in each row.

NAME _____ DATE _____

Standardized Test Practice

For use with pages 10–16

TEST TAKING STRATEGY   **Work as quickly as you can through the easier sections but avoid making careless errors on easy questions.**

1. *Multiple Choice*   What does the symbol $\vec{BC}$ represent?

   Ⓐ   segment *BC*   Ⓑ   line *BC*

   Ⓒ   point *B*   Ⓓ   ray *BC*

   Ⓔ   ray *CB*

Multiple Choice   **In Exercises 2–6, refer to the diagram below.**

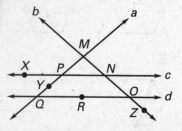

2. Name all points that are collinear to points *N* and *Z*.

   Ⓐ   *P*   Ⓑ   *O*   Ⓒ   *M*

   Ⓓ   *P* and *X*   Ⓔ   *O* and *M*

3. Name a point that lies on line *c*.

   Ⓐ   *M*   Ⓑ   *P*   Ⓒ   *Z*

   Ⓓ   *Q*   Ⓔ   *O*

4. Name all points that are collinear to points *P* and *Q*.

   Ⓐ   *M*   Ⓑ   *N*   Ⓒ   *Y*

   Ⓓ   *X*   Ⓔ   *M* and *Y*

5. Name a point that is coplanar to line *a*.

   Ⓐ   *N*   Ⓑ   *O*   Ⓒ   *R*

   Ⓓ   *Q*   Ⓔ   all of these

6. Name three noncollinear points.

   Ⓐ   *P, Y, Q*   Ⓑ   *M, N, P*   Ⓒ   *M, N, Z*

   Ⓓ   *Q, R, O*   Ⓔ   *X, N, P*

7. *Multiple Choice* $\overleftrightarrow{AB}$ and $\overleftrightarrow{BD}$ intersect at
   ___?___ .

   Ⓐ   *A*   Ⓑ   *B*   Ⓒ   *C*

   Ⓓ   *D*   Ⓔ   none of these

8. *Multiple Choice*   Points *W, X, Y* and *Z* are not coplanar. What is the intersection of plane *WXY* and *WYZ*?

   Ⓐ $\overleftrightarrow{WX}$ Ⓑ $\overleftrightarrow{WY}$ Ⓒ   *W* and *Y*

   Ⓓ   The planes do not intersect.

   Ⓔ   Cannot be determined.

9. *Multi-Step Problem*   Follow the directions below to sketch the figure described.

   a. Draw a plane and three points that lie on the plane that are not collinear. Label the points *A*, *B*, and *C*.

   b. Sketch line segments $\overline{AB}$ and $\overline{BC}$.

   c. Draw a line that intersects plane *ABC* at point *B*. Label the line *l*.

   d. Draw points *D* and *E* on line *l* so that $\vec{BE}$ and $\vec{BD}$ are opposite rays.

NAME _____ DATE _____

Standardized Test Practice

For use with pages 17–25

TEST TAKING STRATEGY   Sketch graphs or figures in your test booklet to help you solve the problems. Even though you must keep your answer sheet neat, you can make any kind of mark you want in your test booklet.

1. *Multiple Choice*   A rule that is accepted without proof is called a ___?___ .

    Ⓐ theorem   Ⓑ postulate

    Ⓒ axiom   Ⓓ A and B

    Ⓔ B and C

2. *Multiple Choice*   Find the length of $\overline{AC}$ if AB is 6, BC is 10, and B is between A and C.

    Ⓐ 4   Ⓑ 16   Ⓒ −4

    Ⓓ 60   Ⓔ 6

Multiple Choice   **In Exercises 3–7, use the diagram below where** $MQ = 30$, $MN = 5$, $MN = NO$, **and** $OP = PQ$.

●————●————●————————●————————●
M   N   O   P   Q

3. Find the length of $\overline{OQ}$.

    Ⓐ 5   Ⓑ 10   Ⓒ 15

    Ⓓ 20   Ⓔ 25

4. Find the length of $\overline{PQ}$.

    Ⓐ 5   Ⓑ 10   Ⓒ 15

    Ⓓ 20   Ⓔ 25

5. Find the length of $\overline{NO}$.

    Ⓐ 5   Ⓑ 10   Ⓒ 15

    Ⓓ 20   Ⓔ 25

6. Find the length of $\overline{NP}$.

    Ⓐ 5   Ⓑ 10   Ⓒ 15

    Ⓓ 20   Ⓔ 25

7. Which of the statements below are not true?

    Ⓐ $NP = MN + PQ$ Ⓑ $MP = OQ$

    Ⓒ $NQ = MP$ Ⓓ $MO = PQ$

    Ⓔ $MQ = PQ \cdot 3$

8. *Multiple Choice*   Point H is between G and I. Use the segment addition postulate to solve for x when $GH = 8x + 7$, $HI = 3x - 2$, and $GI = 38$.

    Ⓐ 3   Ⓑ 5   Ⓒ 7

    Ⓓ 31   Ⓔ 39

9. *Multiple Choice*   In Exercise 8, the length of $\overline{HI}$ is ___?___ .

    Ⓐ 3   Ⓑ 5   Ⓒ 7

    Ⓓ 31   Ⓔ 39

10. *Multiple Choice*   Use points $A(5, 1)$, $B(5, 6)$, $C(1, 4)$ and $D(4, -2)$ to determine which of the following is true.

    Ⓐ $\overline{AB} \cong \overline{BC}$ Ⓑ $\overline{AB} \cong \overline{CD}$

    Ⓒ $\overline{AB} \cong \overline{BD}$ Ⓓ $\overline{AC} \cong \overline{AB}$

    Ⓔ $\overline{BC} \cong \overline{CD}$

Quantitative Comparison   **In Exercises 11–13, choose the statement below that is true about the given values.**

    Ⓐ The value in column A is greater.

    Ⓑ The value in column B is greater.

    Ⓒ The two values are equal.

    Ⓓ The relationship cannot be determined from the information given.

	Column A	Column B
11.	AB when $A(1, 3)$ and $B(3, -6)$	XY when $X(5, 2)$ and $Y(-1, 4)$
12.	AB when $A(-2, -4)$ and $B(3, 2)$	XY when $X(-5, 3)$ and $Y(-8, -2)$
13.	XZ	$XY + YZ$

NAME _____ DATE _____

Standardized Test Practice

For use with pages 26–32

TEST TAKING STRATEGY   **Avoid spending too much time on one question. Skip questions that are too difficult for you, and spend no more than a few minutes on each question.**

1. Multiple Choice   Angle *A* is an obtuse angle for which measure(s)?

Ⓐ $0° < m\angle A < 90°$

Ⓑ $0° < m\angle A < 180°$

Ⓒ $90° < m\angle A < 180°$

Ⓓ $m\angle A = 90°$

Ⓔ $m\angle A = 180°$

2. Multiple Choice   An angle measuring 35° would be a(n) ____?____ .

Ⓐ acute angle   Ⓑ obtuse angle

Ⓒ right angle   Ⓓ straight angle

Ⓔ adjacent angle

3. Multiple Choice   Which angle appears to be a right angle?

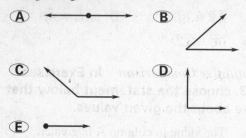

4. Multiple Choice   Find $m\angle WYZ$.

Ⓐ 5°   Ⓑ 90°

Ⓒ 85°   Ⓓ 105°

Ⓔ 175°

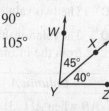

5. Multiple Choice   Find $m\angle BDC$.

Ⓐ 185°

Ⓑ 115°

Ⓒ 25°

Ⓓ 175°

Ⓔ 100°

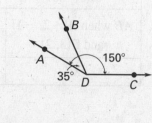

6. Multiple Choice   Plot the points $A(-6, 4)$, $B(-1, 1)$ and $C(3, 1)$ in a coordinate plane. Sketch $\angle ABC$. The angle is a(n) ____?____ .

Ⓐ acute angle   Ⓑ obtuse angle

Ⓒ right angle   Ⓓ straight angle

Ⓔ adjacent angle

7. Multiple Choice   Using the same three points in Exercise 6, sketch $\angle ACB$. The angle is a(n) ____?____ .

Ⓐ acute angle   Ⓑ obtuse angle

Ⓒ right angle   Ⓓ straight angle

Ⓔ adjacent angle

8. Quantitative Comparison   Use the following information.

- *D* is interior to $\angle ABE$ • $m\angle ABD = 50°$
- *E* is interior to $\angle DBF$ • $m\angle EBC = 90°$
- *F* is interior to $\angle EBC$ • $m\angle ABD = m\angle EBF$

Choose the statement below that is true about the given values.

Ⓐ The value in column A is greater.

Ⓑ The value in column B is greater.

Ⓒ The two values are equal.

Ⓓ The relationship cannot be determined from the information given.

Column A	Column B
$m\angle ABC$	$m\angle ABE + m\angle EBC$

Geometry
Standardized Test Practice Workbook

LESSON 1.5

Standardized Test Practice

For use with pages 34–42

TEST TAKING STRATEGY   **Staying physically relaxed during the SAT is very important. If you find yourself tensing up, put your pencil down and take a couple of deep breaths. This will help you stay calm.**

1. *Multiple Choice*   Find the midpoint of a segment with endpoints $A(3, -2)$ and $B(8, 1)$.

Ⓐ $\left(\frac{5}{2}, -\frac{3}{2}\right)$ Ⓑ $\left(\frac{11}{2}, \frac{1}{2}\right)$ Ⓒ $\left(\frac{11}{2}, -\frac{1}{2}\right)$

Ⓓ $\left(\frac{5}{2}, -\frac{1}{2}\right)$ Ⓔ $\left(\frac{11}{2}, -\frac{3}{2}\right)$

2. *Multiple Choice*   Find the midpoint of a segment with endpoints $A(-7, 3)$ and $B(3, -3)$.

Ⓐ $(-2, -3)$ Ⓑ $(-2, 0)$

Ⓒ $(-5, 0)$ Ⓓ $(2, 0)$

Ⓔ $(-5, -3)$

3. *Multiple Choice*   Find the coordinates of the other endpoint of a segment with an endpoint of $X(13, 5)$ and midpoint $M(8, 3)$.

Ⓐ $(18, 7)$ Ⓑ $(18, 1)$

Ⓒ $(3, 7)$ Ⓓ $(3, 1)$

Ⓔ $(-29, -11)$

4. *Multiple Choice*   Find the coordinates of the other endpoint of a segment with an endpoint of $X(-2, 3)$ and midpoint $M(1, -2)$.

Ⓐ $(4, -7)$ Ⓑ $(-4, 7)$

Ⓒ $(0, -1)$ Ⓓ $(-5, 8)$

Ⓔ $(4, 8)$

5. *Multiple Choice*   Choose the congruent angles on the triangle shown.

Ⓐ $\angle A$ and $\angle B$

Ⓑ $\angle A$ and $\angle C$

Ⓒ $\angle B$ and $\angle C$

Ⓓ $\overline{AB}$ and $\overline{AC}$

Ⓔ $\overline{AB}$ and $\overline{BC}$

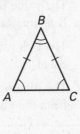

6. *Multiple Choice* $\overrightarrow{BD}$ bisects $\angle ABC$. If the $m\angle DBC = 28°$, what is the $m\angle ABD$?

Ⓐ $14°$ Ⓑ $28°$ Ⓒ $56°$

Ⓓ $62°$ Ⓔ $152°$

7. *Multiple Choice* $\overrightarrow{QS}$ bisects $\angle MQR$. What is the $m\angle MQR$?

Ⓐ $26°$ Ⓑ $52°$

Ⓒ $104°$ Ⓓ $13°$

Ⓔ $38°$

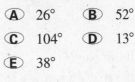

8. *Multiple Choice* $\overrightarrow{AB}$ bisects $\angle CAD$. Find the value of x.

Ⓐ 2 Ⓑ 56

Ⓒ 5 Ⓓ 28

Ⓔ 6

$(8x - 20)°$

$\left(\frac{1}{2}x + 25\right)°$

Quantitative Comparison   In Exercises 9 and 10, use the diagram below where $\overrightarrow{BD}$ bisects $\angle ABC$ and $\overrightarrow{BE}$ bisects $\angle ABD$.

Choose the statement below that is true about the given values.

Ⓐ   The value in column A is greater.

Ⓑ   The value in column B is greater.

Ⓒ   The two values are equal.

Ⓓ   The relationship cannot be determined.

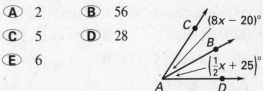

	Column A	Column B
9.	$m\angle ABE + m\angle EBD$	$m\angle DBC$
10.	$m\angle ABD$	$180°$

NAME _____ DATE _____

Standardized Test Practice

For use with pages 44–50

TEST TAKING STRATEGY The mathematical portion of the SAT is based on material taught in your high school mathematics courses. One of the best ways to prepare for the SAT is to keep up with your regular studies and do your homework assignments.

Multiple Choice **Refer to the diagram below for Exercises 1–3.**

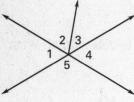

1. Which angles are a linear pair?

Ⓐ ∠1 and ∠2   Ⓑ ∠2 and ∠3

Ⓒ ∠1 and ∠4   Ⓓ ∠4 and ∠5

Ⓔ ∠3 and ∠5

2. Which angles are vertical angles?

Ⓐ ∠1 and ∠2   Ⓑ ∠1 and ∠5

Ⓒ ∠3 and ∠5   Ⓓ ∠1 and ∠4

Ⓔ ∠4 and ∠5

3. Which angles are supplementary?

Ⓐ ∠1 and ∠4   Ⓑ ∠4 and ∠5

Ⓒ ∠1 and ∠5   Ⓓ B and C

Ⓔ all of these

4. *Multiple Choice* Two angles are supplementary. One angle has a measure that is five less than four times the other. What is the measure of the larger angle?

Ⓐ 19   Ⓑ 71   Ⓒ 143

Ⓓ 148   Ⓔ 153

5. *Multiple Choice* What is the $m\angle 1$?

Ⓐ 45°   Ⓑ 90°

Ⓒ 55°   Ⓓ 145°

Ⓔ 155°

6. *Multiple Choice* Find the value of x.

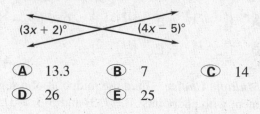

$(3x + 2)°$ $(4x − 5)°$

Ⓐ 13.3   Ⓑ 7   Ⓒ 14

Ⓓ 26   Ⓔ 25

7. *Multiple Choice* Two angles are complementary. One angle has a measure that is twice the other angle. What is the measure of the smaller angle?

Ⓐ 15   Ⓑ 30   Ⓒ 45

Ⓓ 60   Ⓔ 75

8. *Multiple Choice* Find the value of y.

$(4x − 12)°$ $(2x + 8)°$
$(7y + 12)°$

Ⓐ 10   Ⓑ 28   Ⓒ 20

Ⓓ 152   Ⓔ 128

Quantitative Comparison **In Exercises 9 and 10, use the diagram below and choose the statement below that is true about the given value. The $m\angle 3 = 76°$.**

Ⓐ The value in column A is greater.

Ⓑ The value in column B is greater.

Ⓒ The two values are equal.

Ⓓ The relationship cannot be determined from the given information.

	Column A	Column B
9.	$m\angle 3$	$m\angle 1$
10.	$m\angle 4$	The supplement of ∠1

NAME _____ DATE _____

Standardized Test Practice

For use with pages 51–58

TEST TAKING STRATEGY **Make sure you are familiar with the directions before taking a standardized test. This way, you do not need to worry about the directions during the test.**

1. *Multiple Choice* Find the perimeter of the figure.

   Ⓐ 7   Ⓑ 8

   Ⓒ 14   Ⓓ 16

   Ⓔ 30

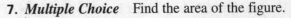

2. *Multiple Choice* Find the circumference of the circle. (Use $\pi \approx 3.14$.)

   Ⓐ 18.84 ft

   Ⓑ 37.68 ft

   Ⓒ 113.04 ft

   Ⓓ 37.68 ft²

   Ⓔ 113.04 ft²

   6 ft

3. *Multiple Choice* Find the area of a square with a side of 7 inches.

   Ⓐ 14 in.   Ⓑ 28 in.²   Ⓒ 49 in.

   Ⓓ 49 in.²   Ⓔ 28 in.

4. *Multiple Choice* Find the area of a triangle with a base of 8 m and a height of 4 m.

   Ⓐ 19 m   Ⓑ 32 m²   Ⓒ 16 m²

   Ⓓ 16 m   Ⓔ 12 m²

5. *Multiple Choice* Find the area of a circle with a radius of 9 meters. (Use $\pi \approx 3.14$.)

   Ⓐ 28.26 m²   Ⓑ 28.26 m

   Ⓒ 56.52 m²   Ⓓ 56.52 m

   Ⓔ 254.34 m²

6. *Multiple Choice* Find the area of the figure.

   Ⓐ 50.24 cm²

   Ⓑ 25.12 cm²

   Ⓒ 401.92 cm²

   Ⓓ 200.96 cm²

   Ⓔ 100.48 cm²

   ⊢—— 16 cm ——⊣

7. *Multiple Choice* Find the area of the figure.

   Ⓐ 18.84 square units

   Ⓑ 9.42 square units

   Ⓒ 28.26 square units

   Ⓓ 56.52 square units

   Ⓔ 88.74 square units

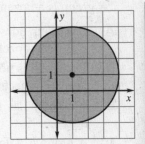

8. *Multiple Choice* Find the area of the rectangle defined by $A(2, 1)$, $B(2, 4)$, $C(6, 4)$ and $D(6, 1)$.

   Ⓐ 7 square units   Ⓑ 14 square units

   Ⓒ 24 square units   Ⓓ 12 square units

   Ⓔ 9 square units

9. *Multiple Choice* A square with an area of 64 square inches has a perimeter of ___?___.

   Ⓐ 64 in.   Ⓑ 16 in.   Ⓒ 32 in.

   Ⓓ 128 in.   Ⓔ cannot be determined

10. *Multiple Choice* A triangle has an area of 72 square feet and a height of 9 feet. Find its base.

    Ⓐ 16 ft   Ⓑ 8 ft   Ⓒ 32 ft

    Ⓓ 9 ft   Ⓔ 34 ft

11. *Multi-Step Problem* A rectangular window pane is 40 inches by 50 inches.

    a. Find the area of the window pane.

    b. Find the perimeter of the window pane.

    c. A frame around the window pane is 1.5 inches wide. Find the area and perimeter of the window pane, including the frame. With the frame, by what percent did the area increase?

Chapter 1

NAME _____ DATE _____

Standardized Test Practice

For use with pages 71–78

TEST TAKING STRATEGY   **When checking your work, try to use a method other than the one you originally used to get your answer. If you use the same method, you may make the same mistake twice.**

1. *Multiple Choice*   What is the if-then form of "A group is a dozen if it has 12 objects?"

   Ⓐ If a group does not have 12 objects, then it is not a dozen.

   Ⓑ If a group is not a dozen, then it does not have 12 objects.

   Ⓒ If a group has 12 objects, then it is a dozen.

   Ⓓ A group is a dozen if and only if it has 12 objects.

   Ⓔ None of the above

2. *Multiple Choice*   What is the inverse of "If water is ice, then the water's temperature is 32°F?"

   Ⓐ If water's temperature is 32°F, then it is ice.

   Ⓑ If water is not ice, then its temperature is not 32°F.

   Ⓒ If water's temperature is not 32°F, then water is not ice.

   Ⓓ Water is ice if and only if its temperature is 32°F.

   Ⓔ None of the above

3. *Multiple Choice*   What is the converse of "If you are hungry, then you did not eat lunch?"

   Ⓐ If you did not eat lunch, then you are hungry.

   Ⓑ If you ate lunch, then you are not hungry.

   Ⓒ If you are not hungry, then you ate lunch.

   Ⓓ You are hungry if and only if you did not eat lunch.

   Ⓔ None of the above

4. *Multiple Choice*   What is the contrapositive of "If $x = 3$, then $5x - 2 = 13$?"

   Ⓐ $5x - 2 = 13$ if and only if $x = 3$.

   Ⓑ If $x \neq 3$, then $5x - 2 \neq 13$.

   Ⓒ If $5x - 2 = 13$, then $x = 3$.

   Ⓓ If $5x - 2 \neq 13$, then $x \neq 3$.

   Ⓔ None of the above

5. *Multiple Choice*   Which of the following statements is not true?

   Ⓐ If $x = 4$, then $x^2 = 16$.

   Ⓑ If $x^3 = -27$, then $x = -3$.

   Ⓒ If $x \neq -3$, then $x^3 \neq -27$.

   Ⓓ If $x = 2$, then $x^2 = 4$.

   Ⓔ If $x^2 = 4$, then $x = 2$.

6. *Multiple Choice*   Use the conditional statement "If an angle is obtuse, then the angle measures 98°" to decide which of the following are true.

   I.   The statement is true.

   II. The converse of the statement is true.

   III. The contrapositive of the statement is true.

   Ⓐ I only   Ⓑ II only

   Ⓒ III only   Ⓓ I and II

   Ⓔ I and III

7. *Multi-Step Problem*   Use Postulate 8 to answer parts (a)–(e).

   Postulate 8: Through any three non-collinear points there exists exactly one plane.

   a. Rewrite Postulate 8 in if-then form.

   b. Write the converse of Postulate 8.

   c. Write the inverse of Postulate 8.

   d. Write the contrapositive of Postulate 8.

   e. *Critical Thinking*   Are the statements you wrote in parts (a)–(d) true?

Standardized Test Practice

For use with pages 79–85

TEST TAKING STRATEGY **If you find yourself spending too much time on one test question and getting frustrated, move to the next question. You can revisit a difficult problem later with a fresh perspective.**

1. *Multiple Choice* Given that $\angle 2 \cong \angle 4$ and $\angle 2 \cong \angle 5$, which statement about the diagram is *not* true?

   Ⓐ $\angle 5 \cong \angle 4$

   Ⓑ $\angle 6$ and $\angle 2$ are supplementary.

   Ⓒ $\angle 8$ and $\angle 5$ are supplementary.

   Ⓓ $\angle 1 \cong \angle 8$

   Ⓔ $\angle 1$ and $\angle 3$ are supplementary.

2. *Multiple Choice* What is the biconditional form of the statement "If a whitetail deer has antlers, then it is a male deer?"

   Ⓐ A whitetail deer has no antlers if and only if it is not a male deer.

   Ⓑ A whitetail deer has antlers if and only if it is a male deer.

   Ⓒ If a whitetail deer has no antlers, then it is not a male deer.

   Ⓓ If a whitetail deer is male, then it has antlers.

   Ⓔ None of the above

3. *Multiple Choice* Which one of the following statements cannot be written as a true biconditional statement?

   Ⓐ If the sum of two angles is 90°, then they are complementary.

   Ⓑ If two angles have the same measurement, then they are congruent.

   Ⓒ If $5x + 7 = 22$, then $x = 3$.

   Ⓓ If two angles are a linear pair, then they are supplementary.

   Ⓔ If Y lies between X and Z, then $XY + YZ = XZ$.

4. *Multiple Choice* Which of the following is true about the conditional statement "If $m\angle 1 = 30°$ and the $m\angle 2 = 150°$, then the angles are supplementary?"

   I.   The statement is true.

   II. The converse is true.

   III. The statement can be written as a true biconditional.

   Ⓐ I   Ⓑ II   Ⓒ III

   Ⓓ I and II   Ⓔ I, II, and III

5. *Multiple Choice* Which statement below would be a true biconditional statement?

   Ⓐ If $\angle ABC$ measures 90°, then it is a right angle.

   Ⓑ If two angles are adjacent, then they share a common side.

   Ⓒ If two squares have the same diagonal length, then they have equal sides.

   Ⓓ A and C

   Ⓔ All of the above

Quantitative Comparison **In Exercises 6 and 7, choose the statement below that is true about the given quantities.**

   Ⓐ The quantity in column A is greater.

   Ⓑ The quantity in column B is greater.

   Ⓒ The two quantities are equal.

   Ⓓ The relationship cannot be determined from the given information.

	Column A	Column B
6.	The number of lines created by the inter-section of two planes	The number of lines that can be drawn through any one point
7.	The sum of two sup-plementary angles	The sum of two adjacent angles

Standardized Test Practice

For use with pages 87–95

TEST TAKING STRATEGY   **It is important to remember that your SAT score will not solely determine your acceptance into a college or university. Do not put added pressure on yourself to do well. If you are not satisfied with your SAT score, remember you can take it again.**

Multiple Choice   For Exercises 1–3, let *p* be "it is raining," let *q* be "it is thundering," and let *r* be "we cannot swim."

1. What is $q \rightarrow p$?

- **A**   If it is raining, then it is thundering.
- **B**   If it is raining, then we cannot swim.
- **C**   If it is thundering, then it is raining.
- **D**   If it is thundering, then we cannot swim.
- **E**   If it is not raining, then it is not thundering.

2. What is the converse of $p \rightarrow q$?

- **A**   If it is thundering, then it is raining.
- **B**   If it is not raining, then it is not thundering.
- **C**   If it is not thundering, then it is not raining.
- **D**   If it is not thundering, then it is raining.
- **E**   If it is thundering, then it is not raining.

3. What is the contrapositive of $r \rightarrow q$?

- **A**   If it is thundering, then we cannot swim.
- **B**   If we can swim, then it is not thundering.
- **C**   If we cannot swim, then it is not thundering.
- **D**   If we can swim, then it is thundering.
- **E**   If it is not thundering, then we can swim.

4. *Multiple Choice*   The statement $\sim p \rightarrow \sim r$ could be ___?___ .

- **A**   the inverse of $r \rightarrow p$
- **B**   the inverse of $\sim r \rightarrow \sim p$
- **C**   the contrapositive of $r \rightarrow p$
- **D**   the converse of $r \rightarrow p$
- **E**   the contrapositive of $\sim r \rightarrow \sim p$

5. *Multiple Choice*   Which type of reasoning allows the conclusion given the true statement? "If it is Saturday, then Nina's family rents movies. Today is Saturday, therefore Nina concludes her family will rent movies."

- **A**   Law of Detachment
- **B**   Law of Syllogism
- **C**   Inductive reasoning
- **D**   Deductive reasoning
- **E**   None of the above

6. *Multiple Choice*   Which type of reasoning allows the conclusion given the true statement? "For the past 4 weeks the ski club has gone skiing on Friday nights. Wendy concludes that the ski club will go skiing this Friday."

- **A**   Law of Detachment
- **B**   Law of Syllogism
- **C**   Inductive reasoning
- **D**   Deductive reasoning
- **E**   None of the above

7. *Multi-Step Problem*   Let *p* be "you get caught exceeding the speed limit," let *q* be "you will get a speeding ticket," and let *r* be "you will pay higher insurance rates."

- **a.** Write $p \rightarrow q$ in words.
- **b.** Write $q \rightarrow r$ in words.
- **c.** Write the contrapositive of $p \rightarrow q$ in words and symbols.
- **d.** *Writing*   Use the Law of Syllogism and the statements from parts (a) and (b) to write a new conditional statement. How does the Law of Detachment apply?

Standardized Test Practice

For use with pages 96–101

TEST TAKING STRATEGY   **Do not panic if you run out of time before answering all of the questions. You can still receive a high test score without answering every question.**

1. *Multiple Choice*   Which property of equality matches the conditional statement "If $AB = BC$ and $BC = CD$, then $AB = CD$?"

  A Addition property

  B Symmetric property

  C Reflexive property

  D Substitution property

  E Transitive property

2. *Multiple Choice*   Which property of equality matches the conditional statement "If $m\angle X = m\angle Z$, then $m\angle Z = m\angle X$?"

  A Addition property

  B Symmetric property

  C Reflexive property

  D Substitution property

  E Transitive property

3. *Multiple Choice*   Solve $5x = -10$, then choose the property that applies to the required step.

  A Substitution property

  B Addition property

  C Division property

  D Distributive property

  E Reflexive property

4. *Multiple Choice*   Solve $x - 7 = 10$, then choose the property that applies to the required step.

  A Substitution property

  B Addition property

  C Division property

  D Distributive property

  E Reflexive property

5. *Multiple Choice*   Which property of equality matches the conditional statement "If $XY + AB = 15$ and $XY = 5$, then $AB = 10$?"

  A Substitution property

  B Addition property

  C Division property

  D Distributive property

  E Reflexive property

6. *Multiple Choice*   Use the Multiplication property of equality to complete "If $m\angle A = 15°$, then $4(m\angle A) = $ ___?___ .

  A 15°   **B** 30°   **C** 45°

  D 60°   **E** 75°

7. *Multi-Step Problem*   In the diagram, $m\angle ABE = m\angle EBC$ and $m\angle EBD = m\angle DBC$.

State a reason that makes each statement true.

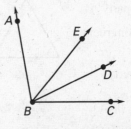

  a. $m\angle EBC = m\angle EBD + m\angle DBC$

  b. $m\angle ABE = m\angle EBC$

  c. $m\angle ABE = m\angle EBD + m\angle DBC$

  d. $m\angle EBD = m\angle DBC$

  e. $m\angle ABE = m\angle EBD + m\angle EBD$

  f. $m\angle ABE = 2(m\angle EBD)$

  g. *Writing*   Use parts (a)–(f) to write an argument for "If $m\angle ABE = m\angle EBC$ and $m\angle EBD = m\angle DBC$, then $m\angle ABE = 2(m\angle EBD)$."

Chapter 2

Standardized Test Practice

For use with pages 102-107

TEST TAKING STRATEGY **Make sure that you are familiar with the directions before taking a standardized test. This way, you do not need to worry about the directions during the test.**

1. *Multiple Choice* In the diagram, $\overline{WX} \cong \overline{YZ}$. Find the length of $\overline{XZ}$.

$$\underset{W}{\overset{5x+1}{\bullet}} \quad \underset{X}{\overset{9x-3}{\bullet}} \quad \underset{Y}{\overset{11}{\bullet}} \quad \underset{Z}{\bullet}$$

  Ⓐ 11   Ⓑ 2   Ⓒ 15

  Ⓓ 4   Ⓔ 26

2. *Multiple Choice* In the diagram, $\overline{AB} \cong \overline{DE}$ and $\overline{BC} \cong \overline{CD}$. Find the length of $\overline{CE}$.

$$\underset{A}{\overset{3x+2}{\bullet}} \quad \underset{B}{\overset{6y-7}{\bullet}} \quad \underset{C}{\overset{y+8}{\bullet}} \quad \underset{D}{\overset{11x-6}{\bullet}} \quad \underset{E}{\bullet}$$

  Ⓐ 11   Ⓑ 22   Ⓒ 10

  Ⓓ 16   Ⓔ 5

3. *Multiple Choice* In $\triangle KLM$, $\overline{KL} \cong \overline{LM}$, and $KL = 8$, and $KM = 8$. Give a reason why $\overline{KL}$ and $\overline{KM}$ are congruent.

  Ⓐ Reflexive property

  Ⓑ Symmetric property

  Ⓒ Definition of congruent segments

  Ⓓ Transitive property

  Ⓔ Addition property

4. *Multiple Choice* In the figure from Exercise 3, $\overline{KL} \cong \overline{LM}$ and $\overline{LM} \cong \overline{KM}$. Give a reason that $\overline{KL} \cong \overline{KM}$.

  Ⓐ Reflexive property

  Ⓑ Transitive property

  Ⓒ Symmetric property

  Ⓓ Definition of congruent segments

  Ⓔ Addition property

5. *Multiple Choice* In $WXYZ$, $\overline{WZ} \cong \overline{XY}$. What is the value of x?

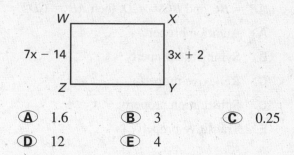

  Ⓐ 1.6   Ⓑ 3   Ⓒ 0.25

  Ⓓ 12   Ⓔ 4

Quantitative Comparison **In Exercises 6–8, use the diagram below to choose the statement that is true about the given values.**

  Ⓐ The value in column A is greater.

  Ⓑ The value in column B is greater.

  Ⓒ The two values are equal.

  Ⓓ The relationship cannot be determined from the given information.

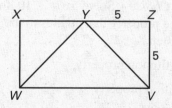

Given: Y is the midpoint of $\overline{XZ}$,
$\overline{XW} \cong \overline{ZV}$, and $\overline{XZ} \cong \overline{WV}$.

	Column A	Column B
6.	XY	YZ
7.	WV	$3(ZV)$
8.	$WV + ZV$	$2(XY) + 2(YZ)$

NAME _____ DATE _____

Standardized Test Practice

For use with pages 109–116

TEST TAKING STRATEGY **Staying physically relaxed during the SAT is very important. If you find yourself tensing up, put your pencil down and take a couple of deep breaths. This will help you stay calm.**

1. *Multiple Choice* Two angles $\angle 1$ and $\angle 2$ are complementary. If $m\angle 1$ is 27°, what is $m\angle 2$?

   (A) 27° (B) 54° (C) 90°

   (D) 63° (E) 153°

2. *Multiple Choice* Two angles, $\angle 1$ and $\angle 2$, are supplementary to $\angle 3$. If $m\angle 1 = 85°$, then $m\angle 1 + m\angle 3 = $ __?__ .

   (A) 85° (B) 170° (C) 90°

   (D) 265° (E) 180°

3. *Multiple Choice* What is $m\angle 2$ if $m\angle 1 = 35°$?

   (A) 35° (B) 70° (C) 90°

   (D) 145° (E) 55°

4. *Multiple Choice* If $m\angle 3 = 126°$, then $m\angle 2 = $ __?__ .

   (A) 63° (B) 64°

   (C) 126° (D) 128°

   (E) 36°

5. *Multiple Choice* Solve for x in the diagram.

   (A) 2 (B) 4

   (C) 8 (D) 16

   (E) 1

   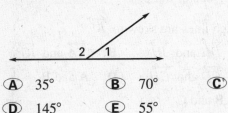

   $(3x + 2)°$ $(13x - 18)°$

6. *Multiple Choice* Solve for y in the diagram.

   (A) 20

   (B) 45

   (C) 51

   (D) 78

   (E) 102

   $(3x + 18)°$

   $(5x + 2)°$ $2(y + 6)°$

7. *Multiple Choice* Given that $\angle 1$ is not a right angle, $\angle 1$ and $\angle 2$ form a linear pair, $\angle 3$ and $\angle 4$ form a linear pair, and $\angle 1$ and $\angle 3$ are vertical angles. Which statement below is *not* true?

   (A) $m\angle 1 + m\angle 4 = 180°$

   (B) $m\angle 3 + m\angle 4 = 180°$

   (C) $\angle 2 \cong \angle 4$

   (D) $m\angle 2 + m\angle 4 = 180°$

   (E) $\angle 1 \cong \angle 3$

Quantitative Comparison **In Exercises 8–10, choose the statement that is true about the diagram. In the diagram,** $\angle 4 \cong \angle 5$, $m\angle 3 = 40°$, $m\angle 6 = 120°$, **and** $m\angle 3 + m\angle 5 + m\angle 9 = 180°$.

   (A) The value in column A is greater.

   (B) The value in column B is greater.

   (C) The two values are equal.

   (D) The relationship cannot be determined from the given information.

	Column A	Column B
8.	$m\angle 1$	$4(m\angle 7)$
9.	$m\angle 9$	$m\angle 11$
10.	$2(m\angle 4)$	$m\angle 10$

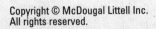

NAME _____ DATE _____

Standardized Test Practice

For use with pages 129–134

TEST TAKING STRATEGY   Work as quickly as you can through the easier sections, but avoid making careless errors on easy questions.

1. *Multiple Choice*   In the diagram, how many lines can be drawn through point *X* that are skew to line *a*?

   Ⓐ 0   Ⓑ 1

   Ⓒ 2   Ⓓ 3

   Ⓔ   More than 3

Multiple Choice   In Exercises 2–5, use the diagram below.

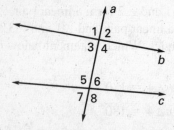

2. Which angles are corresponding angles?

   Ⓐ ∠1 and ∠5   Ⓑ ∠4 and ∠6

   Ⓒ ∠2 and ∠6   Ⓓ A and B

   Ⓔ A and C

3. Which angles are alternate exterior angles?

   Ⓐ ∠2 and ∠8   Ⓑ ∠2 and ∠7

   Ⓒ ∠3 and ∠8   Ⓓ A and B

   Ⓔ A and C

4. Which angles are consecutive interior angles?

   Ⓐ ∠3 and ∠5   Ⓑ ∠4 and ∠6

   Ⓒ ∠3 and ∠7   Ⓓ A and B

   Ⓔ A and C

5. What type of angles are ∠4 and ∠5?

   Ⓐ   Corresponding angles

   Ⓑ   Alternate exterior angles

   Ⓒ   Alternate interior angles

   Ⓓ   Consecutive interior angles

   Ⓔ   Consecutive exterior angles

Multiple Choice   In Exercises 6–8, use the diagram below. Think of each segment as part of a line.

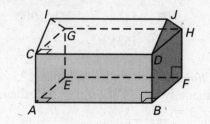

6. $\overleftrightarrow{AC}$ and $\overleftrightarrow{HF}$ are _____?_____.

   Ⓐ   perpendicular   Ⓑ   skew

   Ⓒ   parallel   Ⓓ   intersecting

   Ⓔ   None of these

7. Which lines are skew to $\overleftrightarrow{BF}$?

   Ⓐ $\overleftrightarrow{DH}$ and $\overleftrightarrow{JH}$ Ⓑ $\overleftrightarrow{CA}$ and $\overleftrightarrow{IG}$

   Ⓒ $\overleftrightarrow{CD}$ and $\overleftrightarrow{GH}$ Ⓓ A and B

   Ⓔ B and C

8. Which lines are perpendicular to $\overleftrightarrow{CG}$?

   Ⓐ $\overleftrightarrow{CD}$ and $\overleftrightarrow{CA}$ Ⓑ $\overleftrightarrow{GH}$ and $\overleftrightarrow{EF}$

   Ⓒ $\overleftrightarrow{HF}$ and $\overleftrightarrow{CA}$ Ⓓ A and B

   Ⓔ B and C

9. *Multi-Step Problem*   Use the diagram below to answer parts (a)–(d). Think of each segment as part of a line.

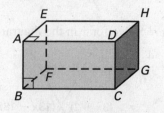

   a. Name all lines parallel to $\overleftrightarrow{AD}$.

   b. Name all lines skew to $\overleftrightarrow{FG}$.

   c. Name all lines perpendicular to $\overleftrightarrow{BF}$.

   d. *Critical Thinking*   If you did not know ∠ABC was a right angle, which answers above would be affected?

Standardized Test Practice

For use with pages 136–141

TEST TAKING STRATEGY **Avoid spending too much time on one question. Skip questions that are too difficult for you, and spend no more than a few minutes on each question.**

1. *Multiple Choice*   Find the value of *x*.

   A 55   **B** 35
   C 90   **D** 145
   E 125

2. *Multiple Choice*   Find the value of *x*.

   A 25   **B** 50
   C 90   **D** 65
   E 155

3. *Multiple Choice*
   Which of the following must be true if $a \perp b$?

   I. $\angle 1$ and $\angle 2$ are complementary.

   II. $m\angle 1 + m\angle 2 < 180°$

   III. $m\angle 1 = m\angle 2$

   A I only   **B** II only
   C I and II   **D** I and III
   E I, II, and III

4. *Multiple Choice*   Find the value of *x*.

   A 35
   B 70
   C 55
   D 110
   E 90

5. *Multiple Choice*   Find the value of *y* from Exercise 4.

   A 35   **B** 70   **C** 55
   D 110   **E** 90

Quantitative Comparison   **For Exercises 6–8, use the diagram below. Choose the statement that is true about the given values.**

   Given: $x \perp y$
   $m\angle 5 = 35°$

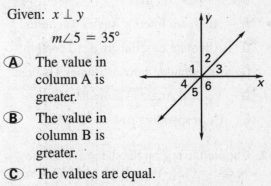

   A   The value in column A is greater.
   B   The value in column B is greater.
   C   The values are equal.
   D   The relationship cannot be determined from the given information.

	Column A	Column B
6.	$m\angle 2 + m\angle 4$	$m\angle 6$
7.	$m\angle 1 + m\angle 2$	$m\angle 3 + m\angle 6$
8.	$m\angle 3$	$m\angle 5$

Chapter 3

Standardized Test Practice
For use with pages 143–149

TEST TAKING STRATEGY Sketch graphs or figures in your test booklet to help you solve the problem. Even though you must keep your answer sheet neat, you can make any kind of mark you want in your test booklet.

Multiple Choice **For Exercises 1–4, use the diagram at the right, where $a \parallel b$.**

1. Choose the reason the statement "If the $m\angle 1 = 65°$, then $m\angle 5 = 65°$ " is true.

- **(A)** Alternate Interior Angles Theorem
- **(B)** Alternate Exterior Angles Theorem
- **(C)** Consecutive Interior Angles Theorem
- **(D)** Vertical Angles Theorem
- **(E)** Corresponding Angles Postulate

2. Choose the reason the statement "If the $m\angle 3 = 115°$, then $m\angle 5 = 65°$ " is true.

- **(A)** Alternate Interior Angles Theorem
- **(B)** Alternate Exterior Angles Theorem
- **(C)** Consecutive Interior Angles Theorem
- **(D)** Vertical Angles Theorem
- **(E)** Corresponding Angles Postulate

3. Choose the reason the statement "If the $m\angle 2 = 115°$, then $m\angle 7 = 115°$ " is true.

- **(A)** Alternate Interior Angles Theorem
- **(B)** Alternate Exterior Angles Theorem
- **(C)** Consecutive Interior Angles Theorem
- **(D)** Vertical Angles Theorem
- **(E)** Corresponding Angles Postulate

4. If the $m\angle 6 = 115°$, then the $m\angle 3 = $ ___?___ .

- **(A)** 65°   **(B)** 115°   **(C)** 180°
- **(D)** 90°   **(E)** cannot be determined

5. *Multiple Choice* Which of the following is *not* true when $a \parallel b$?

- **(A)** $\angle 1 \cong \angle 5$ and $\angle 4 \cong \angle 8$
- **(B)** $m\angle 2 = m\angle 6$
- **(C)** $m\angle 1 + m\angle 5 = 180°$
- **(D)** $m\angle 4 + m\angle 6 = 180°$
- **(E)** $m\angle 4 = m\angle 8$

Quantitative Comparison **In Exercises 6–8, use the diagram below where $a \parallel b$ and $x \parallel y$. Choose the statement that is true about the given values.**

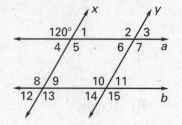

- **(A)** The value in column A is greater.
- **(B)** The value in column B is greater.
- **(C)** The two values are equal.
- **(D)** The relationship cannot be determined from the given information.

	Column A	Column B
6.	$m\angle 2$	$m\angle 8$
7.	$m\angle 10 + m\angle 6$	$m\angle 3 + m\angle 12$
8.	$m\angle 4$	$m\angle 14$

NAME _____ DATE _____

Standardized Test Practice

For use with pages 150–156

TEST TAKING STRATEGY   **When checking your work, try to use a method other than the one you originally used to get your answer. If you use the same method, you may make the same mistake twice.**

1. *Multiple Choice*
   Which postulate or theorem would prove $x \parallel y$?

   Ⓐ Consecutive Interior Angles Converse

   Ⓑ Corresponding Angles Converse

   Ⓒ Alternate Interior Angles Converse

   Ⓓ Alternate Exterior Angles Converse

   Ⓔ Cannot prove $x \parallel y$ with given information

2. *Multiple Choice*
   Which postulate or theorem would prove $a \parallel b$?

   Ⓐ Consecutive Interior Angles Converse

   Ⓑ Corresponding Angles Converse

   Ⓒ Alternate Interior Angles Converse

   Ⓓ Alternate Exterior Angles Converse

   Ⓔ Cannot prove $a \parallel b$ with given information

3. *Multiple Choice*
   Which postulate or theorem would prove $x \parallel y$?

   Ⓐ Consecutive Interior Angles Converse

   Ⓑ Corresponding Angles Converse

   Ⓒ Alternate Interior Angles Converse

   Ⓓ Alternate Exterior Angles Converse

   Ⓔ Cannot prove $x \parallel y$ with given information

4. *Multiple Choice*   What value of x would make lines w and v parallel?

   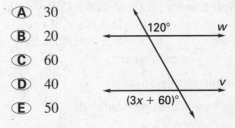

   Ⓐ 30

   Ⓑ 20

   Ⓒ 60

   Ⓓ 40

   Ⓔ 50

5. *Multiple Choice*   Which lines are parallel?

   Ⓐ $\overleftrightarrow{EB} \parallel \overleftrightarrow{FD}$

   Ⓑ $\overleftrightarrow{AE} \parallel \overleftrightarrow{CF}$

   Ⓒ $\overleftrightarrow{EF} \parallel \overleftrightarrow{BC}$

   Ⓓ B and C

   Ⓔ All of the above

6. *Quantitative Comparison*   **Use the diagram below to find the values of x and y that would make $a \parallel b$.**

   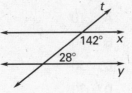

   Choose the statement that is true about the given values.

   Ⓐ The value in column A is greater.

   Ⓑ The value in column B is greater.

   Ⓒ The two values are equal.

   Ⓓ The relationship cannot be determined from the given information.

Column A	Column B
x	y

Chapter 3

NAME _____ DATE _____

Standardized Test Practice

For use with pages 157–164

TEST TAKING STRATEGY **It is important to remember that your SAT score will not solely determine your acceptance into a college or university. Do not put added pressure on yourself to do well. If you are not satisfied with your SAT score, remember that you can take it again.**

1. *Multiple Choice*   Complete the following to make a true statement. "In a plane, if two lines are ___?___ to the same line, then they are ___?___ to each other."

(A) perpendicular, parallel

(B) perpendicular, perpendicular

(C) parallel, parallel

(D) parallel, perpendicular

(E) A and C

2. *Multiple Choice*
Which theorem or postulate shows $j \parallel k$?

(A) Alt. Int. ∠s Converse

(B) Cons. Int. ∠s Converse

(C) Alt. Ext. ∠s Converse

(D) Corresp. ∠s Converse

(E) None of these

3. *Multiple Choice*
Which theorem or postulate shows $j \parallel k$?

(A) Alt. Int. ∠s Converse

(B) Cons. Int. ∠s Converse

(C) Alt. Ext. ∠s Converse

(D) Corresp. ∠s Converse

(E) None of these

4. *Multiple Choice*   Which of the statements must be true if $a \parallel b$ and $x \parallel y$?

I. $m\angle 1 = m\angle 5$

II. $m\angle 3 + m\angle 5 = 180°$

III. $m\angle 7 + m\angle 8 = 180°$

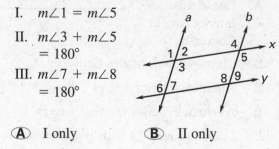

(A) I only   (B) II only

(C) III only   (D) I and III

(E) All of the above

5. *Multiple Choice*   Determine which lines must be parallel.

(A) $a \parallel b$

(B) $c \parallel d$

(C) $c \parallel e$

(D) A and B

(E) A and C

6. *Multiple Choice*   What value of x makes $a \parallel b$?

(A) 10

(B) 30

(C) 50

(D) 70

(E) 90

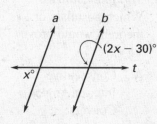

7. *Multi-Step Problem*   Given $a \parallel b$, $m \parallel n$, and $a \perp m$.

a. Prove $a \perp n$.

b. Prove $b \perp n$.

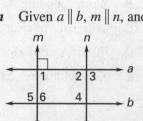

NAME _____ DATE _____

Standardized Test Practice

For use with pages 165–171

TEST TAKING STRATEGY **Read each test question carefully. Always look for short-cuts that will allow you to work through a problem more quickly.**

1. *Multiple Choice* Find the slope of the line that passes through $(5, 2)$ and $(8, -1)$.

   A 1   **B** -1 **C** $-\frac{1}{3}$

   D $\frac{1}{3}$ **E** 2

2. *Multiple Choice* Which equation of the line has a slope of 5 and passes through point $(-2, 1)$?

   A $y = 5x - 11$ **B** $y = 5x - 2$

   C $y = 5x - 9$ **D** $y = 5x + 11$

   E $y = 11x + 5$

3. *Multiple Choice* Which equation of the line has a y-intercept of 6 and is parallel to $y = -\frac{1}{2}x + 2$?

   A $y = -\frac{1}{2}x - 6$ **B** $y = \frac{1}{2}x - 6$

   C $y = -\frac{1}{2}x + 6$ **D** $y = \frac{1}{2}x + 6$

   E $y = 2x + 6$

4. *Multiple Choice* Which equation of the line passes through $(3, -2)$ and is parallel to $y = \frac{2}{3}x$?

   A $y = \frac{2}{3}x - 2$ **B** $y = \frac{2}{3}x + 3$

   C $y = \frac{2}{3}x - 4$ **D** $y = \frac{2}{3}x$

   E $y = \frac{2}{3}x + 4$

5. *Multiple Choice* Which of the following is an equation of a line parallel to $4y - 8 = 3x$?

   A $y = -\frac{3}{4}x + 6$ **B** $y = \frac{4}{3}x + 2$

   C $y = -\frac{4}{3}x - 1$ **D** $y = 3x - 4$

   E $y = \frac{3}{4}x$

6. *Multiple Choice* Which lines are parallel?

   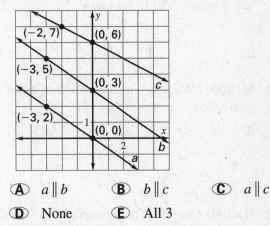

   A $a \parallel b$ **B** $b \parallel c$ **C** $a \parallel c$

   D None   **E** All 3

7. *Multiple Choice* A line k has equation $y = -\frac{2}{3}x + 1$. If $k \parallel i$ and i passes through point $(4, 1)$, what is the equation of i?

   A $y = -\frac{2}{3}x + \frac{11}{3}$ **B** $y = -\frac{3}{2}x + 4$

   C $y = -\frac{2}{3}x + 4$ **D** $y = \frac{2}{3}x + \frac{11}{3}$

   E $y = -\frac{2}{3}x + 1$

Quantitative Comparison **In Exercises 8 and 9, choose the statement below which is true about the given values.**

   A The value in column A is greater.

   B The value in column B is greater.

   C The two values are equal.

   D The relationship cannot be determined from the given information.

	Column A	Column B
8.	The slope of the line passing through $(7, 5)$ and $(4, 6)$	The slope of the line passing through $(7, 3)$ and $(11, 2)$
9.	The y-intercept of $y = \frac{3}{4}x$	The y-intercept of the line passing through $(-1, 2)$ and $(4, -1)$

Chapter 3

Standardized Test Practice
For use with pages 172–178

TEST TAKING STRATEGY   **Do not panic if you run out of time before answering all of the questions. You can still receive a high test score without answering every question.**

1. **Multiple Choice** Which is the slope of a line perpendicular to the line $y = -2x + 6$?

   (A) 2   (B) $\frac{1}{2}$ (C) $-\frac{1}{2}$

   (D) -6 (E) $-\frac{1}{6}$

2. **Multiple Choice** Which equation of a line is perpendicular to $y = -\frac{2}{5}x - \frac{1}{3}$?

   (A) $y = -\frac{2}{5}x + 3$ (B) $y = -\frac{5}{2}x + 2$

   (C) $y = -\frac{5}{2}x + 3$ (D) $y = 3x + 3$

   (E) $y = \frac{5}{2}x + 6$

3. **Multiple Choice** The product of the slopes of two nonvertical perpendicular lines is ____?____.

   (A) 0   (B) 1   (C) -1

   (D) 2   (E) Cannot be determined with given information

4. **Multiple Choice** A line k has equation $y = -\frac{8}{11}x + 3$. If $k \perp l$ and l passes through point $(4, 3)$, what is the equation of line l?

   (A) $y = \frac{11}{8}x - \frac{5}{2}$ (B) $y = \frac{8}{11}x + \frac{1}{11}$

   (C) $y = \frac{8}{11}x + \frac{5}{2}$ (D) $y = -\frac{11}{8}x + \frac{17}{2}$

   (E) $y = \frac{11}{8}x + \frac{17}{2}$

5. **Multiple Choice** A line i has equation $y = \frac{1}{2}x$. If $i \perp j$ and j passes through point $(6, 2)$, what is the equation of j?

   (A) $y = -2x + 14$ (B) $y = -2x - 14$

   (C) $y = -2x - 10$ (D) $y = -2x + 10$

   (E) $y = -\frac{1}{2}x + 10$

6. **Multiple Choice** Which lines are perpendicular?

   (A) $y = \frac{1}{2}x + 6$ (B) $y = 3x + \frac{1}{3}$
       $y = -\frac{1}{2}x + 1$ $y = 5x - 3$

   (C) $y = \frac{2}{3}x + 3$ (D) $y = 2x + 3$
       $y = -\frac{3}{2}x - 1$ $y = \frac{1}{2}x - 2$

   (E) None of these

7. **Multiple Choice** Which of the following statements are true about lines w, n, p, and z?

   w: $y = \frac{3}{2}x + 2$

   n: $y = \frac{2}{3}x + 6$

   p: $y = -\frac{3}{2}x - 3$

   z: $y = \frac{2}{3}x + 1$

   I. $w \perp p$ II. $n \parallel z$ III. $z \perp p$

   (A) I only   (B) II only

   (C) III only   (D) I and II

   (E) II and III

8. **Multi-Step Problem**

   a. On a coordinate plane, plot points $A(2, 1)$ and $B(5, 2)$.

   b. Find the equation of the line j passing through points A and B.

   c. Find the equation of the line k, perpendicular to line j and passing through point A.

   d. Find the equation of the line l, parallel to line k and passing through point B.

   e. **Critical Thinking** If the bottom of a rectangle lies along line j, and its sides lie on lines k and l, find the slope of the line representing the top.

NAME _____ DATE _____

Standardized Test Practice

For use with pages 194–201

TEST TAKING STRATEGY   **If you find yourself spending too much time on one test question and getting frustrated, move on to the next question. You can revisit a difficult problem later with a fresh perspective.**

1. *Multiple Choice*   A triangle with three acute angles and no congruent sides is ___?___.

   Ⓐ   an equiangular triangle
   Ⓑ   a right triangle
   Ⓒ   an isosceles triangle
   Ⓓ   an obtuse triangle
   Ⓔ   an acute scalene triangle

2. *Multiple Choice*   A triangle with side lengths of 5 cm, 3 cm, and 5 cm is ___?___.

   Ⓐ   an equilateral triangle
   Ⓑ   an obtuse triangle
   Ⓒ   an isosceles triangle
   Ⓓ   an acute triangle
   Ⓔ   a scalene triangle

3. *Multiple Choice*   The triangle below can be classified as ___?___.

   Ⓐ   acute isosceles
   Ⓑ   acute scalene
   Ⓒ   obtuse isosceles
   Ⓓ   obtuse scalene
   Ⓔ   right scalene

   95°

4. *Multiple Choice*   The triangle below can be classified as ___?___.

   Ⓐ   acute isosceles
   Ⓑ   acute scalene
   Ⓒ   obtuse isosceles
   Ⓓ   obtuse scalene
   Ⓔ   right scalene

   35°
   35°

5. *Multiple Choice*   An isosceles triangle has a perimeter of 82 cm. The lengths of the legs of the triangle are represented by $(3x + 2)$ and $(5x - 14)$. Find the length of the base of the triangle.

   Ⓐ   8 cm   Ⓑ   16 cm   Ⓒ   26 cm
   Ⓓ   30 cm   Ⓔ   52 cm

6. *Multiple Choice*   Find the measure of ∠BCD.

   Ⓐ   50°
   Ⓑ   120°
   Ⓒ   60°
   Ⓓ   160°
   Ⓔ   20°

   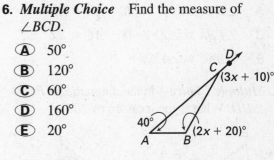

7. *Multiple Choice*   Find the measure of ∠1.

   Ⓐ   40°
   Ⓑ   70°
   Ⓒ   80°
   Ⓓ   140°
   Ⓔ   Cannot be determined

   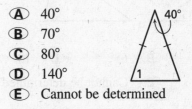

8. *Multiple Choice*   Find the measure of ∠1.

   Ⓐ   50°
   Ⓑ   90°
   Ⓒ   60°
   Ⓓ   30°
   Ⓔ   85°

   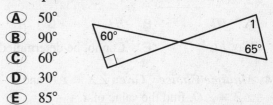

9. *Quantitative Comparison*   **Choose the statement below which is true about the given number.**

   Ⓐ   The value in column A is greater.
   Ⓑ   The value in column B is greater.
   Ⓒ   The two values are equal.
   Ⓓ   The relationship cannot be determined from the given information.

   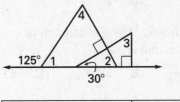

Column A	Column B
$m\angle 1$	$m\angle 2$

NAME _____ DATE _____

Standardized Test Practice

For use with pages 202–210

TEST TAKING STRATEGY   **One of the best ways to prepare for the SAT is to keep up with your regular studies and do your homework.**

1. *Multiple Choice*   If $\triangle ABC \cong \triangle XYZ$, which of the following statements below is *not* true?

- Ⓐ $\angle B \cong \angle Y$
- Ⓑ $\overline{AB} \cong \overline{XY}$
- Ⓒ $\angle CBA \cong \angle ZXY$
- Ⓓ $\overline{AC} \cong \overline{XZ}$
- Ⓔ $\angle BAC \cong \angle YXZ$

2. *Multiple Choice*   In the diagram, $\triangle EFG \cong \triangle HIJ$. What is the measure of $\angle H$?

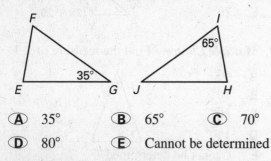

- Ⓐ 35°
- Ⓑ 65°
- Ⓒ 70°
- Ⓓ 80°
- Ⓔ Cannot be determined

3. *Multiple Choice*   In the diagram in Exercise 2, $EG =$ ___?___ .

- Ⓐ HI
- Ⓑ HJ
- Ⓒ JI
- Ⓓ FG
- Ⓔ Cannot be determined

4. *Multiple Choice*   Given $\angle X \cong \angle N$ and $\angle Z \cong \angle O$, find the value of x.

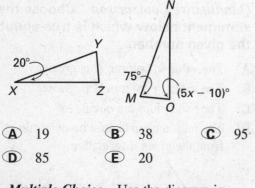

- Ⓐ 19
- Ⓑ 38
- Ⓒ 95
- Ⓓ 85
- Ⓔ 20

5. *Multiple Choice*   Use the diagram in Exercise 4 to find $m\angle Z$.

- Ⓐ 19°
- Ⓑ 38°
- Ⓒ 95°
- Ⓓ 85°
- Ⓔ 20°

6. *Multiple Choice*   Given $\angle M \cong \angle B$ and $\angle K \cong \angle C$, find the value of x.

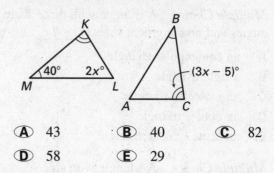

- Ⓐ 43
- Ⓑ 40
- Ⓒ 82
- Ⓓ 58
- Ⓔ 29

Quantitative Comparison   **In Exercises 7 and 8, use the given information to find the indicated value. Choose the statement below that is true about the given value.**

- Ⓐ The value in column A is greater.
- Ⓑ The value in column B is greater.
- Ⓒ The two values are equal.
- Ⓓ The relationship cannot be determined from the given information.

Given: $ABCD \cong EFGH$

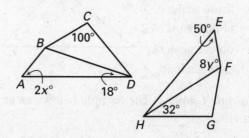

	Column A	Column B
7.	x	y
8.	$m\angle CBD$	$m\angle GHE$

Geometry
Standardized Test Practice Workbook

NAME _____ DATE _____

Standardized Test Practice

For use with pages 212–219

TEST TAKING STRATEGY   **Work as quickly as you can through the easier sections, but avoid making careless errors on easy questions.**

1. Multiple Choice   Use the diagram below. Which additional congruence is needed to prove $\triangle ABC \cong \triangle DEF$?

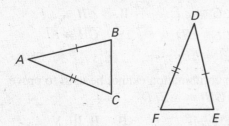

(A) $\angle B \cong \angle E$; SAS Congruence Postulate
(B) $\overline{BC} \cong \overline{FE}$; SSS Congruence Postulate
(C) $\angle A \cong \angle D$; SAS Congruence Postulate
(D) A or B
(E) B or C

2. Multiple Choice   Use the diagram below. Which congruence is needed to prove $\triangle XYZ \cong \triangle JKL$?

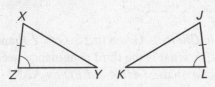

(A) $\angle Y \cong \angle K$; SAS Congruence Postulate
(B) $\overline{XY} \cong \overline{JK}$; SAS Congruence Postulate
(C) $\overline{ZY} \cong \overline{LK}$; SAS Congruence Postulate
(D) A or B
(E) B or C

Multiple Choice   **Use the following choices to complete the proofs that $\triangle AED \cong \triangle CDE$ and $\triangle ABE \cong \triangle DBC$. Given: B is the midpoint of $\overline{EC}$ and $\overline{AD}$.**

(A) Given
(B) Def. of midpoint
(C) Reflexive Prop. of Congruence
(D) SSS Congruence Postulate
(E) SAS Congruence Postulate

Statements	Reasons
a. $\overline{AE} \cong \overline{CD}$	a. 3. _____
b. $\angle AED \cong \angle CDE$	b. 4. _____
c. $\overline{ED} \cong \overline{ED}$	c. 5. _____
d. $\triangle AED \cong \triangle CDE$	d. 6. _____

Statements	Reasons
e. B is the midpoint of $\overline{AD}$ and $\overline{EC}$.	e. 7. _____
f. $\overline{BC} \cong \overline{BE}$, $\overline{AB} \cong \overline{BD}$	f. 8. _____
g. $\triangle ABE \cong \triangle DBC$	g. 9. _____

10. Multiple Choice   In rectangle $ABCD$, a diagonal is drawn from B to D. Which statement is not true?

(A) $\angle DAB \cong \angle BCD$ (B) $\angle ABD \cong \angle CDB$
(C) $\overline{AB} \cong \overline{BC}$ (D) $\overline{DB} \cong \overline{DB}$
(E) $\angle ADB \cong \angle CBD$

11. Multiple Choice   In $\triangle MNO$ and $\triangle XYZ$, $\overline{MN} \cong \overline{XY}$ and $\overline{NO} \cong \overline{YZ}$. If the triangles are congruent, what else must be true?

(A) $\angle N \cong \angle Y$ (B) $\angle M \cong \angle Z$
(C) $\overline{MO} \cong \overline{XZ}$ (D) A and C
(E) All of the above

12. Multi-Step Problem

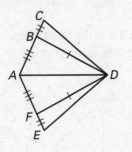

a. Prove that $\triangle ADF \cong \triangle ADB$.
b. Prove that $\triangle ACD \cong \triangle AED$.
c. Prove that $\triangle BCD \cong \triangle FED$.

NAME _____ DATE _____

Standardized Test Practice

For use with pages 220–227

TEST TAKING STRATEGY   **Do not panic if you run out of time before answering all of the questions. You can still receive a high test score without answering every question.**

1. *Multiple Choice*   Which postulate or theorem can be used to prove that $\triangle ABC \cong \triangle BAD$?

   (A)   SSS
   (B)   SAS
   (C)   ASA
   (D)   AAS
   (E)   none of the above

2. *Multiple Choice*   Which postulate or theorem can be used to prove that $\triangle EFG \cong \triangle IHG$?

   (A)   SSS   (B)   SAS   (C)   ASA
   (D)   AAS   (E)   none of the above

3. *Multiple Choice*   What is the third congruence needed to prove that $\triangle ABD \cong \triangle CBD$ by AAS?

   (A) $\overline{AB} \cong \overline{BC}$
   (B) $\angle ABD \cong \angle CBD$
   (C) $\overline{AD} \cong \overline{DC}$
   (D) $\angle DBA \cong \angle CDB$
   (E)   B or C

4. *Multiple Choice*   What is the third congruence needed to prove that $\triangle MNQ \cong \triangle PNO$ by ASA?

   (A) $\angle Q \cong \angle P$
   (B) $\angle MNQ \cong \angle PNO$
   (C) $\angle M \cong \angle O$
   (D) $\angle M \cong \angle P$
   (E) $\overline{QN} \cong \overline{NO}$

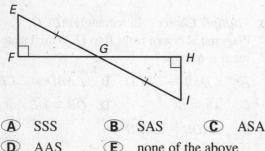

5. *Multiple Choice*   You are given the following information about $\triangle GHI$ and $\triangle EFD$.

   I. $\angle G \cong \angle E$ II. $\angle H \cong \angle F$
   III. $\angle I \cong \angle D$ IV. $\overline{GH} \cong \overline{EF}$
   V. $\overline{GI} \cong \overline{ED}$

   Which combination cannot be used to prove that $\triangle GHI \cong \triangle EFD$?

   (A)   V, IV, II   (B)   II, III, V
   (C)   III, V, I   (D)   V, IV, I
   (E)   none of the above

6. *Multiple Choice*   Given that $\angle X \cong \angle D$, and $\overline{DE} \cong \overline{XW}$, what is the third congruence needed to prove that $\triangle XWY \cong \triangle DEC$ by ASA?

   (A) $\angle Y \cong \angle C$ (B) $\angle Y \cong \angle E$
   (C) $\angle W \cong \angle C$ (D) $\angle W \cong \angle E$
   (E)   none of the above

7. *Multiple Choice*   Given that $\angle G \cong \angle E$ and $\angle I \cong \angle D$, what is the third congruence needed to prove that $\triangle GHI \cong \triangle EFD$ by AAS?

   (A) $\angle H \cong \angle F$ (B) $\overline{HI} \cong \overline{ED}$
   (C) $\overline{HI} \cong \overline{FD}$ (D) $\overline{ED} \cong \overline{GI}$
   (E)   none of the above

8. *Multi-Step Problem*   In the diagram, $\overline{AB} \parallel \overline{CD}$, $\overline{CB} \parallel \overline{DE}$, and $\overline{AB} \cong \overline{CD}$.

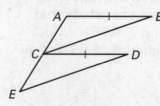

   a. Prove that $\triangle ABC \cong \triangle CDE$.
   b. Prove that C is the midpoint of $\overline{AE}$.

TEST TAKING STRATEGY **Make sure that you are familiar with the directions before taking a standardized test. This way, you do not need to worry about the directions during the test.**

1. *Multiple Choice* Which postulate or theorem can be used to prove that the triangles are congruent given *M* is the midpoint of $\overline{KQ}$ and $\overline{KL} \parallel \overline{PQ}$?

   Ⓐ SSS
   Ⓑ SAS
   Ⓒ ASA
   Ⓓ AAS
   Ⓔ AAA

2. *Multiple Choice* Which statement correctly describes the congruence of the triangles in Exercise 1?

   Ⓐ $\triangle KML \cong \triangle PQM$
   Ⓑ $\triangle KLM \cong \triangle PQM$
   Ⓒ $\triangle KML \cong \triangle QMP$
   Ⓓ $\triangle KLM \cong \triangle PMQ$
   Ⓔ $\triangle KML \cong \triangle MQP$

3. *Multiple Choice* After proving the triangles congruent in Exercise 1, what reason could you give to prove $\overline{KL} \cong \overline{PQ}$?

   Ⓐ Vertical Angles Theorem
   Ⓑ Reflexive Prop. of Congruence
   Ⓒ Corresp. parts of ≅ △ are ≅.
   Ⓓ ASA
   Ⓔ Definition of midpoint

4. *Multiple Choice* You want to prove $\overline{BC} \cong \overline{AF}$. As a first step, which pair of triangles would you prove congruent?

   Ⓐ $\triangle ADF \cong \triangle CDB$
   Ⓑ $\triangle ADF \cong \triangle EDF$
   Ⓒ $\triangle BCD \cong \triangle FED$
   Ⓓ B or C
   Ⓔ Any of the above

Multiple Choice In Exercises 5–13, use the choices below to complete the proof that $\overline{AG} \cong \overline{FE}$.

   Ⓐ Alternate Interior Angles Theorem
   Ⓑ ASA Congruence Postulate
   Ⓒ Corresp. parts of ≅ △ are ≅.
   Ⓓ Vertical Angles Theorem
   Ⓔ Definition of Congruence

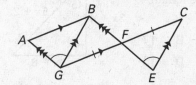

Statements	Reasons
a. $\overline{AB} \parallel \overline{GC}$, $\overline{GB} \parallel \overline{EC}$, $\overline{AG} \parallel \overline{BE}$, $\overline{GF} \cong \overline{FC}$, $\angle AGB \cong \angle FEC$	a. Given
b. $\angle BFG \cong \angle EFC$	b. 5. _____
c. $\angle BGF \cong \angle ECF$	c. 6. _____
d. $\triangle BGF \cong \triangle ECF$	d. 7. _____
e. $\overline{BG} \cong \overline{EC}$	e. 8. _____
f. $\angle ABG \cong \angle FGB$	f. 9. _____
g. $m\angle ABG = m\angle FGB$, $m\angle BGF = m\angle ECF$	g. 10. _____
h. $m\angle ABG = m\angle ECF$	h. Sub. prop. of equality
i. $\angle ABG \cong \angle ECF$	i. 11. _____
j. $\triangle ABG \cong \triangle FCE$	j. 12. _____
k. $\overline{AG} \cong \overline{FE}$	k. 13. _____

14. *Multi-Step Problem* In the diagram, $\angle 1 \cong \angle 3$ and $\angle 2 \cong \angle 4$.

   a. Prove that $\triangle AGC \cong \triangle AGE$.
   b. Prove that $\triangle BCG \cong \triangle FEG$.
   c. Prove that $\triangle CDG \cong \triangle EDG$.

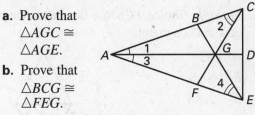

Standardized Test Practice

For use with pages 236–242

Avoid spending too much time on one question. Skip questions that are too difficult for you, and spend no more than a few minutes on each question.

1. *Multiple Choice* What is the value of *x*?

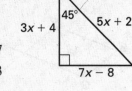

  Ⓐ 3
  Ⓑ 5
  Ⓒ 7
  Ⓓ 9
  Ⓔ 11

2. *Multiple Choice*
What is the length
of a leg?

  Ⓐ 3   Ⓑ 17
  Ⓒ 12 Ⓓ 13
  Ⓔ 19

3. *Multiple Choice* What are the values of *x* and *y*?

  Ⓐ $x = 72.5, y = 72.5$
  Ⓑ $x = 35, y = 35$
  Ⓒ $x = 35, y = 110$
  Ⓓ $x = 55, y = 55$
  Ⓔ $x = 110, y = 35$

4. *Multiple Choice* What is the value of *x*?

  Ⓐ 30
  Ⓑ 60
  Ⓒ 90
  Ⓓ 100
  Ⓔ Cannot be
      determined

5. *Multiple Choice* Choose the reason the triangles are congruent.

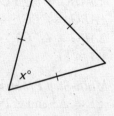

  Ⓐ SSS
  Ⓑ SAS
  Ⓒ AAS
  Ⓓ ASA
  Ⓔ Cannot be proven
      congruent

6. *Multiple Choice* Solve for *x* and *y*.

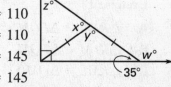

  Ⓐ $x = 120,$
      $y = 60$
  Ⓑ $x = 60,$
      $y = 60$
  Ⓒ $x = 30,$
      $y = 120$
  Ⓓ $x = 120, y = 30$
  Ⓔ $x = 60, y = 120$

7. *Multiple Choice* Solve for *x* and *y*.

  Ⓐ $x = 70, y = 55$
  Ⓑ $x = 55, y = 110$
  Ⓒ $x = 70, y = 110$
  Ⓓ $x = 70, y = 145$
  Ⓔ $x = 55, y = 145$

8. *Multiple Choice* Use the diagram in Exercise 7 to solve for *w* and *z*.

  Ⓐ $w = 145, z = 70$ Ⓑ $w = 110, z = 55$
  Ⓒ $w = 110, z = 70$ Ⓓ $w = 145, z = 55$
  Ⓔ $w = 70, z = 55$

9. *Quantitative Comparison*
**Use the diagram
to find the
missing values.
Choose the state-
ment below that
is true about
the given values.**

  Ⓐ The value in column A is greater.
  Ⓑ The value in column B is greater.
  Ⓒ The two values are equal.
  Ⓓ The relationship cannot be determined
      from the given information.

Column A	Column B
$m\angle 1$	$m\angle 3$

NAME _____ DATE _____

Standardized Test Practice

For use with pages 243–250

1. *Multiple Choice*   An isosceles right triangle has a vertex at $(0, 0)$ and another at $(0, 8)$. If its legs are 8 units, what point below *might* be the third vertex?

   Ⓐ $(8, 0)$ Ⓑ $(-8, 0)$

   Ⓒ $(0, -8)$ Ⓓ A or B

   Ⓔ All of the above

2. *Multiple Choice*   A rectangle with sides of 3 units and 6 units is placed on a coordinate plane. If one vertex is at $(0, 0)$, which set of points could be the other vertex points?

   Ⓐ $(0, 6), (6, 3), (3, 6)$

   Ⓑ $(3, 0), (0, 6), (3, 6)$

   Ⓒ $(-3, 0), (-3, 6), (0, -6)$

   Ⓓ $(3, 0), (0, -6), (-3, -6)$

   Ⓔ All of the above

3. *Multiple Choice*   A right triangle has legs of 8 units and 10 units. Use a coordinate plane to solve for the hypotenuse.

   Ⓐ $\sqrt{18}$ Ⓑ $4\sqrt{5}$ Ⓒ $2\sqrt{41}$

   Ⓓ 80   Ⓔ $3\sqrt{2}$

4. *Multiple Choice*   A rectangle with length h and width k is placed in a coordinate plane with one vertex at $(0, 0)$. What is a possible point for the vertex diagonal to $(0, 0)$?

   Ⓐ $(0, h)$ Ⓑ $(h, 0)$ Ⓒ $(0, -k)$

   Ⓓ $(h, -k)$ Ⓔ $(-h, 0)$

5. *Multiple Choice*   Use the diagram in Exercise 6 to find the length of $\overline{MP}$. M is the midpoint of $\overline{PQ}$.

   Ⓐ 25   Ⓑ 50   Ⓒ 40

   Ⓓ 30   Ⓔ 125

6. *Multiple Choice*   What are the coordinates of the midpoint M?

   Ⓐ $(40, 30)$

   Ⓑ $(60, 40)$

   Ⓒ $(30, 80)$

   Ⓓ $(60, 30)$

   Ⓔ $(30, 40)$

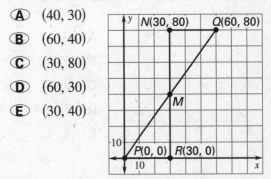

Quantitative Comparison   **In Exercises 7 and 8, use the diagram below. Choose the statement below that is true about the given value.**

   Ⓐ The value in column A is greater.

   Ⓑ The value in column B is greater.

   Ⓒ The two values are equal.

   Ⓓ The relationship cannot be determined from the given information.

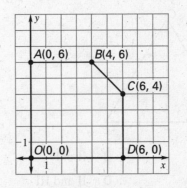

	Column A	**Column B**
7.	AD	$BC + CD$
8.	OB	OC

NAME _____ DATE _____

Standardized Test Practice

For use with pages 264–271

TEST TAKING STRATEGY   Make sure that you are familiar with the directions before taking a standardized test. This way, you do not need to worry about the directions during the test.

1. *Multiple Choice* In the diagram, $\overleftrightarrow{WY}$ is the perpendicular bisector of $\overline{AB}$. What is the value of *x*?

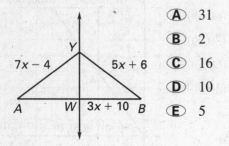

  (A) 31
  (B) 2
  (C) 16
  (D) 10
  (E) 5

2. *Multiple Choice* Which diagram below allows you to conclude that *C* is on the perpendicular bisector of $\overline{AB}$?

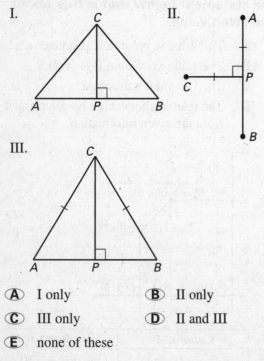

I.

II.

III.

  (A) I only   (B) II only
  (C) III only   (D) II and III
  (E) none of these

3. *Multiple Choice* In the diagram, $\overleftrightarrow{KM} \perp \overleftrightarrow{OQ}$, and $\overline{OP} \cong \overline{PQ}$. Find *PQ*.

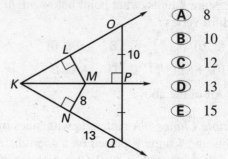

  (A) 8
  (B) 10
  (C) 12
  (D) 13
  (E) 15

4. *Multiple Choice* In the diagram, in Exercise 3, $\overrightarrow{KM}$ bisects $\angle OKQ$. Find *LM*.

  (A) 8   (B) 10   (C) 12
  (D) 13   (E) 15

Quantitative Comparison **In Exercises 5 and 6, choose the statement below that is true about the given values.**

  (A) The value in column A is greater.

  (B) The value in column B is greater.

  (C) The two values are equal.

  (D) The relationship cannot be determined from the given information.

Given: $\overrightarrow{MN}$ is the perpendicular bisector of $\overline{AB}$.

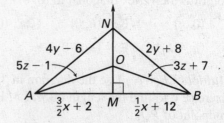

	Column A	Column B
5.	AB	NB
6.	AN	AO

LESSON
5.2

NAME _____ DATE _____

Standardized Test Practice

For use with pages 272–278

TEST TAKING STRATEGY **Work as quickly as you can through the easier sections, but avoid making careless errors on easy questions.**

1. *Multiple Choice* Complete the statement so that it is true. "The point of concurrency of the _____ of a triangle is called the _____ of the triangle."

   Ⓐ perpendicular bisectors; incenter

   Ⓑ perpendicular bisectors; circumcenter

   Ⓒ angle bisectors; circumcenter

   Ⓓ angle bisectors; inscribecenter

   Ⓔ A and C

2. *Multiple Choice* In the diagram, P is the circumcenter of $\triangle ABC$. Find the value of x.

   Ⓐ 1

   Ⓑ 3

   Ⓒ 9

   Ⓓ 15

   Ⓔ 21

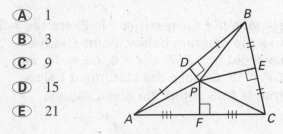

Given: $PB = 15$; $PC = 3x + 6$

3. *Multiple Choice* The point of concurrency of the three perpendicular bisectors of an obtuse triangle is __?__ the triangle.

   Ⓐ always inside   Ⓑ always outside

   Ⓒ always on   Ⓓ sometimes inside

   Ⓔ sometimes outside

4. *Multiple Choice* The point of concurrency of the three angle bisectors of a right triangle is __?__ the triangle.

   Ⓐ always inside   Ⓑ always outside

   Ⓒ always on   Ⓓ sometimes inside

   Ⓔ sometimes on

5. *Multiple Choice* In the diagram, the angle bisectors of $\triangle ACE$ meet at point G. Find GD.

   Ⓐ 1

   Ⓑ 2

   Ⓒ 3

   Ⓓ 4

   Ⓔ 5

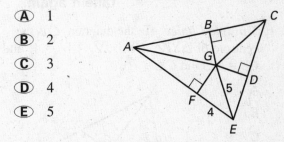

6. *Multiple Choice* In the diagram below, the angle bisectors of $\triangle KLM$ meet at point N. Find NP.

   Ⓐ 10

   Ⓑ 25

   Ⓒ 20

   Ⓓ 31

   Ⓔ 15

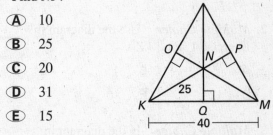

7. *Multi-Step Problem* A city is planning a new recreational park. They want to locate the new park so that it is equidistant from three large apartment complexes.

a. What term best describes the point the city is looking for?

b. The three apartment complexes would be located at $(4, 5)$, $(2, 1)$, and $(6, 1)$ on a coordinate plane. Plot the points and draw the perpendicular bisectors of the triangle formed.

c. What are the coordinates of the best position for the new park?

d. If each unit on the coordinate plane is 1 mile, how far is each apartment complex from the park?

LESSON
5.3

Chapter 5

NAME _____ DATE _____

Standardized Test Practice

For use with pages 279–285

TEST TAKING STRATEGY   It is important to remember that your SAT score will not solely determine your acceptance into a college or university. Do not put added pressure on yourself to do well. If you are not satisfied with your SAT score, remember that you can take it again.

1. *Multiple Choice*   In the diagram, C is the centroid of $\triangle XYZ$, $\overline{UY} \perp \overline{XZ}$, $CW = 4$, and $CZ = 8$. Find CX.

   (A) 3

   (B) 6

   (C) 9

   (D) 8

   (E) 12

2. *Multiple Choice*   Use the diagram in Exercise 1. Find VZ.

   (A) $\frac{16}{3}$ (B) 4   (C) 8

   (D) 12   (E) 16

3. *Multiple Choice*   In the diagram in Exercise 1, $\overline{UY}$ is ? .

   (A) an altitude

   (B) a perpendicular bisector

   (C) a median

   (D) an angle bisector   (E) all of these

4. *Multiple Choice*   What are the coordinates of the centroid of a triangle whose vertices are $A(3, 1)$, $B(7, 3)$, and $C(5, 7)$?

   (A) $\left(5, \frac{11}{3}\right)$ (B) $\left(5, \frac{16}{3}\right)$ (C) $(5, 2)$

   (D) $\left(6, \frac{8}{3}\right)$ (E) $\left(6, \frac{11}{3}\right)$

5. *Multiple Choice*   What is the area of $\triangle ABC$?

   (A) 50

   (B) 48

   (C) 51

   (D) 42

   (E) 320

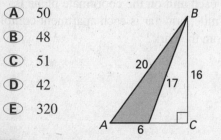

6. *Multiple Choice*   Complete the statement so that it is true. "The three altitudes of an obtuse triangle ? intersect ? the triangle."

   (A) always; inside

   (B) sometimes; inside

   (C) always; outside

   (D) sometimes; outside

   (E) never; outside

Quantitative Comparison   In Exercises 7–9, use the diagram below. Point *C* is the centroid of $\triangle DEF$, $CH = 6$, $GE = 10$, and $GF = 15$. Choose the statement below that is true about the given values.

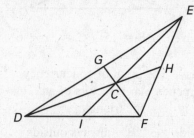

   (A) The value in column A is greater.

   (B) The value in column B is greater.

   (C) The two values are equal.

   (D) The relationship cannot be determined from the given information.

	Column A	Column B
7.	DE	DH
8.	GC	CF
9.	CE	CD

LESSON

5.4

NAME _____ DATE _____

Standardized Test Practice

For use with pages 287–293

Chapter 5

TEST TAKING STRATEGY   **Do not panic if you run out of time before answering all of the questions. You can still receive a high test score without answering every question.**

1. *Multiple Choice*   In the diagram, $\overline{UV}$ and $\overline{WU}$ are midsegments of $\triangle XYZ$. Find *WX*.

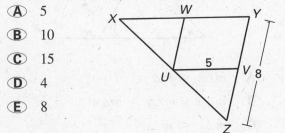

  Ⓐ   5

  Ⓑ   10

  Ⓒ   15

  Ⓓ   4

  Ⓔ   8

2. *Multiple Choice*   Use the diagram in Exercise 1 to find *WU*.

  Ⓐ   5   Ⓑ   10   Ⓒ   15

  Ⓓ   4   Ⓔ   8

3. *Multiple Choice*   Find the coordinates of the endpoints of the midsegment parallel to $\overline{AB}$.

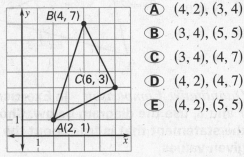

  Ⓐ   (4, 2), (3, 4)

  Ⓑ   (3, 4), (5, 5)

  Ⓒ   (3, 4), (4, 7)

  Ⓓ   (4, 2), (4, 7)

  Ⓔ   (4, 2), (5, 5)

4. *Multiple Choice*   Given the midpoints of a triangle are (7, 4), (5, 6) and (8, 7), which coordinates below are the vertices?

  Ⓐ   (6, 9), (5, 4), (11, 6)

  Ⓑ   (5, 4), (10, 5), (6, 9)

  Ⓒ   (4, 3), (10, 5), (6, 9)

  Ⓓ   (4, 3), (7, 9), (11, 5)

  Ⓔ   (4, 3), (6, 9), (11, 6)

5. *Multiple Choice*   Use the diagram to find the perimeter of $\triangle KLM$.

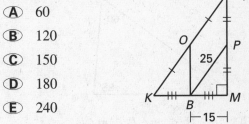

  Ⓐ   60

  Ⓑ   120

  Ⓒ   150

  Ⓓ   180

  Ⓔ   240

6. *Multiple Choice*   Use the diagram below to find *FG*.

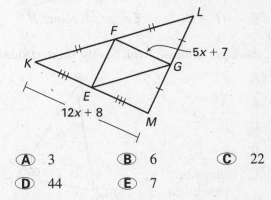

  Ⓐ   3   Ⓑ   6   Ⓒ   22

  Ⓓ   44   Ⓔ   7

Quantitative Comparison   In Exercises 7 and 8, use the diagram below. $\overline{BD}$, $\overline{DF}$, and $\overline{BF}$ are midsegments of $\triangle ACE$.
BC = 10, AE = 12. Choose the statement below that is true about the given value.

  Ⓐ   The value in column A is greater.

  Ⓑ   The value in column B is greater.

  Ⓒ   The two values are equal.

  Ⓓ   The relationship cannot be determined from the given information.

	Column A	Column B
7.	*BD*	*BF*
8.	The perimeter of $\triangle CDB$	The perimeter of $\triangle DEF$

Standardized Test Practice

For use with pages 295–301

1. *Multiple Choice*   Use the diagram below to determine which statement is true.

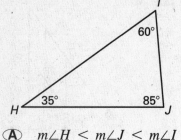

Ⓐ $m\angle H < m\angle J < m\angle I$

Ⓑ $HI < HJ < JI$

Ⓒ $JI < HJ < HI$

Ⓓ $HJ > HI$ Ⓔ $m\angle I < m\angle H$

2. *Multiple Choice*   Which is the shortest side?

Ⓐ $\overline{AC}$

Ⓑ $\overline{AB}$

Ⓒ $\overline{BC}$

Ⓓ   A or C

Ⓔ   cannot be determined

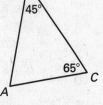

3. *Multiple Choice*   List the sides in order from longest to shortest.

Ⓐ $\overline{GF}, \overline{EF}, \overline{EG}$

Ⓑ $\overline{EG}, \overline{GF}, \overline{EF}$

Ⓒ $\overline{EF}, \overline{EG}, \overline{GF}$

Ⓓ $\overline{EF}, \overline{GF}, \overline{EG}$

Ⓔ $\overline{EG}, \overline{EF}, \overline{GF}$

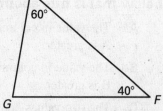

4. *Multiple Choice*   A triangle has two sides that have lengths of 8 cm and 14 cm. Which length below could *not* represent the length of the third side?

Ⓐ   7 cm   Ⓑ   13 cm   Ⓒ   18 cm

Ⓓ   22 cm   Ⓔ   15 cm

5. *Multiple Choice*   Which statement below is false?

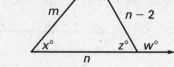

Ⓐ $m\angle x < m\angle y$

Ⓑ $m\angle x + m\angle y > m\angle w$

Ⓒ $m\angle y < m\angle w$

Ⓓ $m\angle x < m\angle w$

Ⓔ $m\angle w > m\angle z$

6. *Multiple Choice*   Use the diagram to solve the inequality $AB + BC > AC$.

Ⓐ $x > 0$

Ⓑ $x < -4$

Ⓒ $x < 0$

Ⓓ $x > 10$

Ⓔ $x > -4$

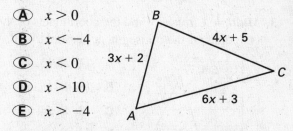

Quantitative Comparison   **In Exercises 7 and 8, use the diagram below. Choose the statement that is true about the given values.**

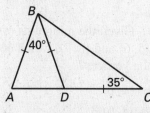

Ⓐ   The value in column A is greater.

Ⓑ   The value in column B is greater.

Ⓒ   The two values are equal.

Ⓓ   The relationship cannot be determined from the given information.

	Column A	Column B
7.	AB	AD
8.	BC	DC

NAME _____ DATE _____

Standardized Test Practice

For use with pages 302–308

TEST TAKING STRATEGY **When checking your work, try to use a method other than the one you originally used to get your answer. If you use the same method, you may make the same mistake twice.**

1. *Multiple Choice* Use the diagram to determine which of the following is a possible length for $\overline{AC}$.

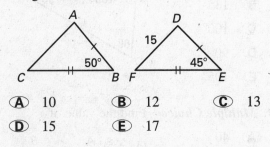

  Ⓐ 10   Ⓑ 12   Ⓒ 13

  Ⓓ 15   Ⓔ 17

2. *Multiple Choice* In the diagram, which of the following is *not* a possible measure for ∠*DCB*?

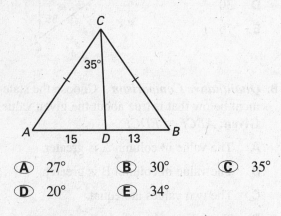

  Ⓐ 27°   Ⓑ 30°   Ⓒ 35°

  Ⓓ 20°   Ⓔ 34°

3. *Multiple Choice* Use the Hinge Theorem and the diagram below to choose the statement which must be true.

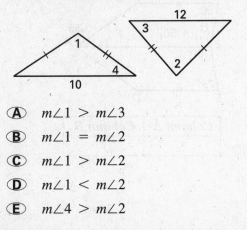

  Ⓐ $m\angle 1 > m\angle 3$

  Ⓑ $m\angle 1 = m\angle 2$

  Ⓒ $m\angle 1 > m\angle 2$

  Ⓓ $m\angle 1 < m\angle 2$

  Ⓔ $m\angle 4 > m\angle 2$

4. *Multiple Choice* Use the diagram below and the given information to choose the conclusion that is true.

  Given: $\overline{AB} \cong \overline{ED}$, $\overline{AC} \cong \overline{CD}$,
        $EC > BC$

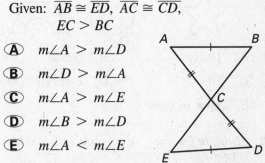

  Ⓐ $m\angle A > m\angle D$

  Ⓑ $m\angle D > m\angle A$

  Ⓒ $m\angle A > m\angle E$

  Ⓓ $m\angle B > m\angle D$

  Ⓔ $m\angle A < m\angle E$

5. *Multiple Choice* Use the diagram and the Hinge Theorem to choose the inequality that correctly describes the restriction on the value of *x*.

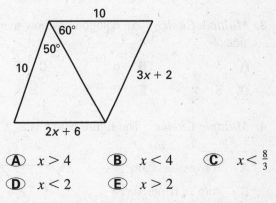

  Ⓐ $x > 4$ Ⓑ $x < 4$ Ⓒ $x < \frac{8}{3}$

  Ⓓ $x < 2$ Ⓔ $x > 2$

6. *Multi-Step Problem*

  a. Sketch an acute triangle *ABC* with $m\angle A = 45°$ and $m\angle C = 55°$.

  b. Draw an exterior angle adjacent to ∠*BCA* with vertex at *C*, and label it ∠*BCD*.

  c. Determine $m\angle BCD$.

  d. What is the shortest side of △*ABC*?

  e. Use your diagram as a reference to write the first statement of an indirect proof of "the measure of an exterior angle of a triangle is equal to the sum of the two non-adjacent interior angles."

Standardized Test Practice

For use with pages 322–328

TEST TAKING STRATEGY   Do not panic if you run out of time before answering all of the questions. You can still receive a high test score without answering every question.

1. Multiple Choice   Which figure below is a polygon?

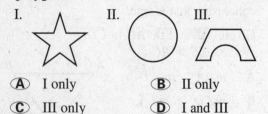

I.   II.   III.

Ⓐ   I only   Ⓑ   II only

Ⓒ   III only   Ⓓ   I and III

Ⓔ   none of these

2. Multiple Choice   A polygon with 7 sides is called a ___?___ .

Ⓐ   nonagon   Ⓑ   dodecagon

Ⓒ   heptagon   Ⓓ   hexagon

Ⓔ   decagon

3. Multiple Choice   An octagon has how many sides?

Ⓐ   5   Ⓑ   6   Ⓒ   7

Ⓓ   8   Ⓔ   9

4. Multiple Choice   The figure below is a ___?___ .

Ⓐ   convex hexagon

Ⓑ   convex heptagon

Ⓒ   concave heptagon

Ⓓ   concave hexagon

Ⓔ   concave pentagon

5. Multiple Choice   The polygon below is best described as ___?___ .

Ⓐ   an equilateral pentagon

Ⓑ   an equiangular pentagon

Ⓒ   a regular pentagon

Ⓓ   an equilateral hexagon

Ⓔ   an equiangular hexagon

6. Multiple Choice   Find $m\angle A$.

Ⓐ   65°

Ⓑ   135°

Ⓒ   100°

Ⓓ   90°

Ⓔ   105°

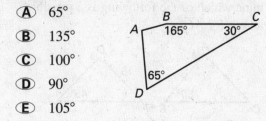

7. Multiple Choice   Find the value of x.

Ⓐ   40

Ⓑ   10

Ⓒ   45

Ⓓ   30

Ⓔ   70

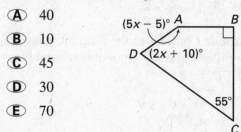

8. Quantitative Comparison   Choose the statement below that is true about the given value.

Given: $ABCF \cong EDCF$

Ⓐ   The value in column A is greater.

Ⓑ   The value in column B is greater.

Ⓒ   The two values are equal.

Ⓓ   The relationship cannot be determined from the given information.

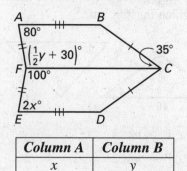

Column A	Column B
x	y

Geometry
Standardized Test Practice Workbook

Standardized Test Practice

For use with pages 330–337

TEST TAKING STRATEGY   **If you find yourself spending too much time on one test question and getting frustrated, move on to the next question. You can revisit a difficult problem later with a fresh perspective.**

1. **Multiple Choice**   Opposite angles of a parallelogram must be ____?____.

   Ⓐ   complementary   Ⓑ   supplementary

   Ⓒ   congruent   Ⓓ   A and C

   Ⓔ   B and C

2. **Multiple Choice**   What are the values of the variables in parallelogram *ABCD*?

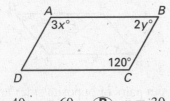

   Ⓐ $x = 40, y = 60$ Ⓑ $x = 30, y = 40$

   Ⓒ $x = 60, y = 20$ Ⓓ $x = 20, y = 60$

   Ⓔ $x = 40, y = 30$

3. **Multiple Choice**   What is the length of $\overline{LP}$?

   Ⓐ   4   Ⓑ   5

   Ⓒ   8   Ⓓ   10

   Ⓔ   20

4. **Multiple Choice**   In the parallelogram in Exercise 3, what is the length of $\overline{MN}$ if the perimeter is 70 units?

   Ⓐ   20 units   Ⓑ   15 units

   Ⓒ   10 units   Ⓓ   30 units

   Ⓔ   50 units

5. **Multiple Choice**   Which statement is not always true about parallelogram *WXYZ*?

   Ⓐ $\overline{VX} \cong \overline{VZ}$

   Ⓑ $\overline{XY} \cong \overline{WZ}$

   Ⓒ $\angle WXY \cong \angle YZW$

   Ⓓ $\overline{WY} \cong \overline{XZ}$

   Ⓔ $\angle WXZ \cong \angle XZY$

6. **Multiple Choice**
   What are the values of *x* and *y*?

   Ⓐ $x = 12, y = 6$ Ⓑ $x = 6, y = 12$

   Ⓒ $x = 8, y = 15$ Ⓓ $x = 4, y = 8$

   Ⓔ $x = 15, y = 8$

7. **Multiple Choice**   Three coordinate points of a parallelogram are (2, 1), (4, 4), and (7, 4). Find the fourth vertex.

   Ⓐ   (5, 1)   Ⓑ   (2, 7)   Ⓒ   (5, 4)

   Ⓓ   (5, 7)   Ⓔ   (1, 7)

8. **Quantitative Comparison**   Use the information given. Choose the statement below that is true about the given value.

   Ⓐ   The value in column A is greater.

   Ⓑ   The value in column B is greater.

   Ⓒ   The two values are equal.

   Ⓓ   The relationship cannot be determined from the given information.

   Given: *ABCD*, *DEFG*, and *FHIJ* are parallelograms.

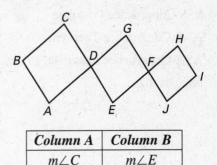

Column A	Column B
$m\angle C$	$m\angle E$

Standardized Test Practice

For use with pages 338–346

TEST TAKING STRATEGY **Read each test question carefully. Always look for shortcuts that will allow you to work through a problem more quickly.**

1. *Multiple Choice* Which additional piece of information do you need to prove *ABCD* is a parallelogram?

   Ⓐ $\overline{AB} \cong \overline{DC}$

   Ⓑ $\overline{AD} \cong \overline{BC}$

   Ⓒ $\overline{AB} \parallel \overline{DC}$

   Ⓓ A or B

   Ⓔ B or C

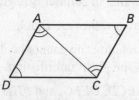

2. *Multiple Choice* *WXYZ* is a quadrilateral. Which information would *not* allow you to conclude that *WXYZ* is a parallelogram?

   Ⓐ $\overline{WX} \cong \overline{ZY}, \overline{WZ} \cong \overline{XY}$

   Ⓑ $\angle W \cong \angle Y, \angle X \cong \angle Z$

   Ⓒ $\overline{WX} \parallel \overline{ZY}, \overline{WZ} \cong \overline{XY}$

   Ⓓ $\overline{WZ} \parallel \overline{XY}, \overline{WX} \parallel \overline{ZY}$

   Ⓔ $\overline{WZ} \cong \overline{XY}, \overline{WZ} \parallel \overline{XY}$

3. *Multiple Choice* To prove that *ABCD* is a parallelogram, you would have to first prove $\triangle ACD \cong \triangle CAB$ using the ___?___ .

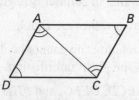

   Ⓐ SAS Congruence Postulate

   Ⓑ SSS Congruence Postulate

   Ⓒ AAS Congruence Theorem

   Ⓓ ASA Congruence Postulate

   Ⓔ none of these

4. *Multiple Choice* What value of *x* will make the quadrilateral a parallelogram?

   Ⓐ 5   Ⓑ 10

   Ⓒ 50   Ⓓ 40

   Ⓔ 60

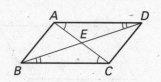

5. *Multiple Choice* Given that $\triangle AED \cong \triangle CEB$, *ABCD* would be a parallelogram because ___?___ .

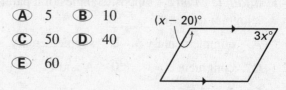

   Ⓐ both pairs of opposite sides are parallel

   Ⓑ the diagonals bisect each other

   Ⓒ both pairs of opposite sides are congruent

   Ⓓ both pairs of opposite angles are congruent

   Ⓔ one angle is supplementary to both of its consecutive angles

6. *Multi-Step Problem* Consider the four points $A(5, 4)$, $B(6, 2)$, $C(3, 1)$, and $D(8, 5)$.

   a. Show that *ACBD* is a parallelogram by showing that opposite sides are parallel.

   b. Show that *ACBD* is a parallelogram by showing that opposite sides are congruent.

   c. Show that *ACBD* is a parallelogram by showing that the diagonals bisect each other. Label the intersection of diagonals $\overline{AB}$ and $\overline{CD}$ point *E*.

NAME_____ DATE _____

Standardized Test Practice

For use with pages 347–355

TEST TAKING STRATEGY   **When checking your work, try to use a method other than the one you originally used to get your answer. If you use the same method, you may make the same mistake twice.**

1. *Multiple Choice*   What special type of quadrilateral has the vertices $A(-2, 1)$, $B(2, -3)$, $C(2, 1)$, and $D(-2, -3)$?

  (A) rhombus   **(B)** square

  (C) rectangle   **(D)** parallelogram

  (E) none of these

2. *Multiple Choice* $WXYZ$ is a rhombus. What is the value of x?

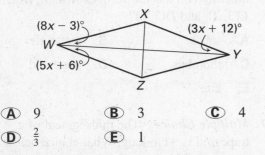

  (A) 9   **(B)** 3   **(C)** 4

  (D) $\frac{2}{3}$ **(E)** 1

3. *Multiple Choice*   In the diagram below, $PQRS$ is a rhombus. What are the values of x and y?

  (A) $x = \frac{5}{3}, y = 4$

  (B) $x = 5, y = 2$

  (C) $x = 10, y = 4$

  (D) $x = 5, y = 6$

  (E) $x = 10, y = 6$

4. *Multiple Choice*   The diagonals of a rectangle must ____?____.

  (A) bisect each other   **(B)** be perpendicular

  (C) be congruent   **(D)** A and B

  (E) A and C

5. *Multiple Choice*   If a quadrilateral has four equal sides, then it must be a ____?____.

  (A) rectangle   **(B)** square

  (C) rhombus   **(D)** A and B

  (E) B and C

6. *Multiple Choice*   In rectangle $ABCD$, $AB = \frac{1}{2}x + 6$ and $CD = \frac{5}{2}x - 2$. Find the value of x.

  (A) 4   **(B)** $\frac{3}{4}$ **(C)** 5

  (D) 2   **(E)** $\frac{3}{3}$

7. *Multiple Choice*   The perimeter of a square $MNOP$ is 72 inches, and $NO = 2x + 6$. What is the value of x?

  (A) 15   **(B)** 12   **(C)** 6

  (D) 9   **(E)** 18

8. *Multiple Choice* $KLMN$ is a rectangle. Find the values of x and y.

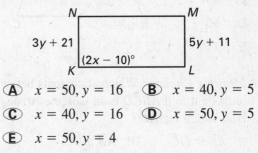

  (A) $x = 50, y = 16$ **(B)** $x = 40, y = 5$

  (C) $x = 40, y = 16$ **(D)** $x = 50, y = 5$

  (E) $x = 50, y = 4$

Quantitative Comparison
In the diagram, $ACEG$ is a rhombus, $BDFH$ is a rectangle, and $\triangle ACE$ is an equilateral triangle. For Exercises 9 and 10, choose a statement below that is true about the given values.

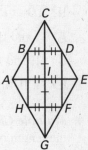

  (A) The value in column A is greater.

  (B) The value in column B is greater.

  (C) The two values are equal.

  (D) The relationship cannot be determined from the given information.

	Column A	Column B
9.	$m\angle BAI$	$m\angle ICD$
10.	BC	GF

NAME _____ DATE _____

Standardized Test Practice

For use with pages 356–363

TEST TAKING STRATEGY **Staying physically relaxed during the SAT is very important. If you find yourself tensing up, put your pencil down and take a couple of deep breaths. This will help you stay calm.**

1. *Multiple Choice*   In trapezoid *KLMN*, $\overline{KL}$ and $\overline{NM}$ are ___?___ .

Ⓐ legs

Ⓑ bases

Ⓒ consecutive angles

Ⓓ diagonals

Ⓔ none of these

2. *Multiple Choice*   In the isosceles trapezoid *ABCD*, find $m\angle B$.

Ⓐ 110°

Ⓑ 55°

Ⓒ 70°

Ⓓ 60°

Ⓔ 140°

3. *Multiple Choice*   Which statements below must be true if *ABCD* is an isosceles trapezoid with a leg $\overline{AD}$?

I. $\overline{AB} \cong \overline{DC}$ III. $\overline{AB} \parallel \overline{DC}$

II. $\overline{AD} \cong \overline{BC}$ IV. $\overline{AD} \parallel \overline{BC}$

Ⓐ I and III   Ⓑ I and IV

Ⓒ II and III   Ⓓ II and IV

Ⓔ I, II, and III

4. *Multiple Choice*   *ABCD* is a trapezoid. Find the length of midsegment $\overline{EF}$.

Ⓐ 5

Ⓑ 11

Ⓒ 16

Ⓓ 8

Ⓔ 22

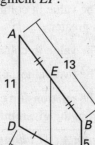

5. *Multiple Choice*   Find the length of $\overline{KL}$ in the trapezoid below.

Ⓐ 22   Ⓑ 4

Ⓒ 13   Ⓓ 17

Ⓔ 27

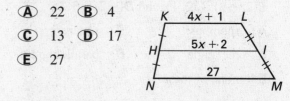

6. *Multiple Choice*   What special type of quadrilateral has the vertices $A(6, 3)$, $B(2, 5)$, $C(3, 2)$, and $D(5, 6)$?

Ⓐ square   Ⓑ rectangle

Ⓒ rhombus   Ⓓ trapezoid

Ⓔ kite

7. *Multiple Choice*   The midsegment of a trapezoid is 9 cm long. What choice below is *not* a possible choice for the lengths of the bases?

Ⓐ 2, 16   Ⓑ 5, 4   Ⓒ 8, 10

Ⓓ 6, 12   Ⓔ 5, 13

8. *Quantitative Comparison*   In the diagram, *DEFG* is a kite. Choose the statement below that is true about the given value.

Ⓐ The value in column A is greater.

Ⓑ The value in column B is greater.

Ⓒ The values are equal.

Ⓓ The relationship cannot be determined with the given information.

Column A	Column B
x	y

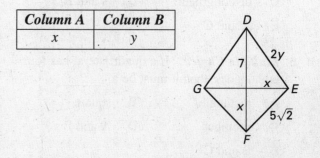

Geometry
Standardized Test Practice Workbook

NAME _____ DATE _____

Standardized Test Practice

For use with pages 364–370

TEST TAKING STRATEGY Avoid spending too much time on one question. Skip questions that are too difficult for you, and spend no more than a few minutes on each question.

1. *Multiple Choice* The quadrilateral below is most specifically a _____?_____.

Ⓐ rhombus

Ⓑ rectangle

Ⓒ kite

Ⓓ parallelogram

Ⓔ trapezoid

2. *Multiple Choice* A quadrilateral with at least two sides parallel and two congruent sides might be _____?_____.

Ⓐ a rhombus

Ⓑ an isosceles trapezoid

Ⓒ a kite

Ⓓ A or B

Ⓔ none of these

3. *Multiple Choice* What kind of quadrilateral would meet the conditions of the diagram? *ABCD* is not drawn to scale.

Ⓐ kite

Ⓑ rhombus

Ⓒ trapezoid

Ⓓ square

Ⓔ parallelogram

4. *Multiple Choice* What value of *x* would make quadrilateral *ABCD* a trapezoid?

Ⓐ 30 Ⓑ 20

Ⓒ 25 Ⓓ 35

Ⓔ 10

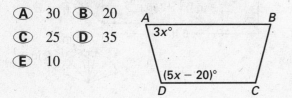

5. *Multiple Choice* Which statements below are always true about a rectangle?

  I. Both pairs of opposite angles are congruent.

 II. The diagonals are perpendicular.

III. Both pairs of opposite sides are congruent.

Ⓐ I Ⓑ II Ⓒ III

Ⓓ I and III Ⓔ none of these

6. *Multiple Choice* Which statements below are always true about a trapezoid?

  I. Exactly one pair of opposite sides are congruent.

 II. Exactly one pair of opposite sides are parallel.

III. The diagonals are congruent.

Ⓐ I Ⓑ II Ⓒ III

Ⓓ I and II Ⓔ none of these

7. *Multi-Step Problem* In the diagram, *DEFG* is a rectangle and △*ABC* is regular.

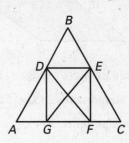

a. If $GE = 10y - 2$ and $DF = \frac{2}{3}y + 12$, find the value of *y*.

b. If the midsegment of trapezoid *DECG* is 5 inches, $DE = 3x + 2$, and $GC = 8x - 3$, find the value of *x*.

c. Prove that △*ADG* ≅ △*CEF*.

Chapter 6

TEST TAKING STRATEGY One of the best ways to prepare for the SAT is to keep up with your regular studies and do your homework.

1. *Multiple Choice* Find the area of a square with a perimeter of 30 cm.

Ⓐ 225 cm²   Ⓑ 15 cm²

Ⓒ 30 cm²   Ⓓ 56.25 cm²

Ⓔ 60 cm²

2. *Multiple Choice* Find the area of △ABC.

Ⓐ 17.5 square units

Ⓑ 7.5 square units

Ⓒ 30 square units

Ⓓ 15 square units

Ⓔ 9 square units

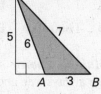

3. *Multiple Choice* Find the base length of a triangle with an area of 52 cm² and a height of 13 cm.

Ⓐ 8 cm   Ⓑ 16 cm   Ⓒ 4 cm

Ⓓ 2 cm   Ⓔ 26 cm

4. *Multiple Choice* Find the area of parallelogram *EFGH*.

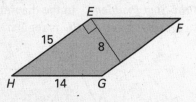

Ⓐ 75 square units   Ⓑ 112 square units

Ⓒ 120 square units   Ⓓ 56 square units

Ⓔ 60 square units

5. *Multiple Choice* The area of the rectangle is 60 square units. Find the value of x.

Ⓐ $\frac{2}{3}$ Ⓑ 40

Ⓒ 59   Ⓓ 7

Ⓔ 8

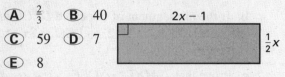

6. *Multiple Choice* The area of the kite is 160 square inches. Find the length of $\overline{BD}$.

Ⓐ 10 in.

Ⓑ 20 in.

Ⓒ 8 in.

Ⓓ 16 in.

Ⓔ 32 in.

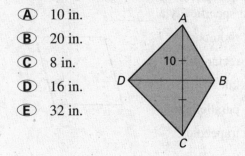

7. *Multiple Choice* Find the area of a trapezoid with vertices at A(0, 0), B(2, 4), C(6, 4), and D(9, 0).

Ⓐ 26 square units   Ⓑ 13 square units

Ⓒ 52 square units   Ⓓ 36 square units

Ⓔ 18 square units

8. *Multi-Step Problem* A doll house is sketched below. There is no back to the house or roof, but there are sides to both.

a. Find the area of the walls (including the windows and the doors).

b. Find the area of the window openings. The window above the door consists of 5 congruent isosceles triangles.

c. Find the area of the roof.

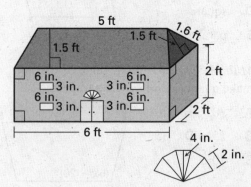

Geometry
Standardized Test Practice Workbook

Cumulative Standardized Test Practice

For use after Chapters 1–6

1. **Multiple Choice** $\overleftrightarrow{XY}$ and $\overleftrightarrow{WY}$ intersect at __?__ .

   Ⓐ   point X Ⓑ   point Y

   Ⓒ   point W Ⓓ $\overline{WX}$

   Ⓔ   none of these

2. **Multiple Choice**   Point B is between A and C. Use the Segment Addition Postulate to solve for x when $AB = 5x + 2$, $AC = 12x + 7$, and $BC = 26$.

   Ⓐ   1   Ⓑ   2   Ⓒ   3

   Ⓓ   4   Ⓔ   5

3. **Multiple Choice**   Find the measure of $\angle ABD$.

   Ⓐ   30°

   Ⓑ   60°

   Ⓒ   90°

   Ⓓ   120°

   Ⓔ   150°

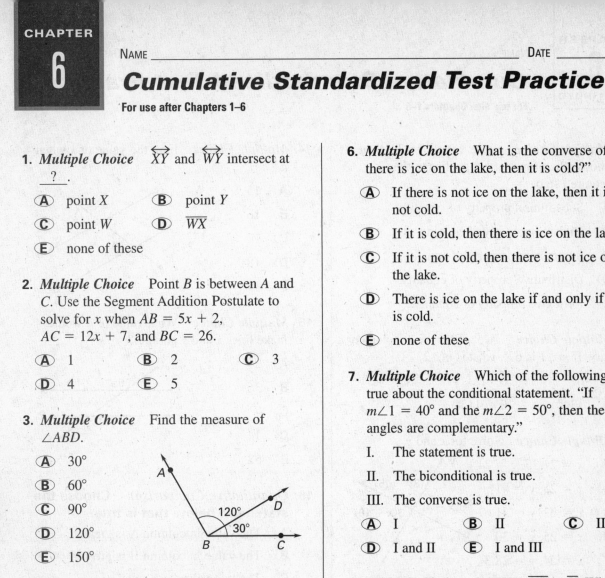

4. **Multiple Choice** $\overrightarrow{AB}$ bisects $\angle CAD$. Find the value of x.

   Ⓐ   2

   Ⓑ   4

   Ⓒ   6

   Ⓓ   8

   Ⓔ   10

5. **Multiple Choice**   Find the value of y.

   Ⓐ   30

   Ⓑ   35

   Ⓒ   85

   Ⓓ   22

   Ⓔ   55

6. **Multiple Choice**   What is the converse of "If there is ice on the lake, then it is cold?"

   Ⓐ   If there is not ice on the lake, then it is not cold.

   Ⓑ   If it is cold, then there is ice on the lake.

   Ⓒ   If it is not cold, then there is not ice on the lake.

   Ⓓ   There is ice on the lake if and only if it is cold.

   Ⓔ   none of these

7. **Multiple Choice**   Which of the following is true about the conditional statement. "If $m\angle 1 = 40°$ and the $m\angle 2 = 50°$, then the angles are complementary."

   I.   The statement is true.

   II.   The biconditional is true.

   III. The converse is true.

   Ⓐ   I   Ⓑ   II   Ⓒ   III

   Ⓓ   I and II   Ⓔ   I and III

8. **Multiple Choice**   In $HIJK$, $\overline{HK} \cong \overline{IJ}$. What is the value of x?

   Ⓐ   1

   Ⓑ   2

   Ⓒ   2.5

   Ⓓ   3

   Ⓔ   3.5

   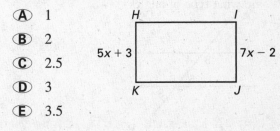

9. **Multi-Step Problem**   Let p be "You stay up late," q be "You are tired" and r be "You are cranky."

   a. Write $p \rightarrow q$ in words.

   b. Write $q \rightarrow r$ in words.

   c. Write the contrapositive of $p \rightarrow q$ in words and symbols.

   d. *Writing*   Use the Law of Syllogism and the statements from parts (a) and (b) to write a new conditional statement.

Chapter 6

10. *Multiple Choice*   Solve $x + 12 = 24$, then choose the property that applies to the required step.

- Ⓐ   Substitution property of equality.
- Ⓑ   Division property of equality.
- Ⓒ   Subtraction property of equality.
- Ⓓ   Distributive property of equality.
- Ⓔ   Reflexive property of equality.

11. *Multiple Choice*   Two angles are supplementary. If $m\angle 1$ is $67°$, what is $m\angle 2$?

- Ⓐ $67°$ Ⓑ $23°$ Ⓒ $46°$
- Ⓓ $134°$ Ⓔ $113°$

12. *Multiple Choice*   Solve for x and y.

- Ⓐ $x = 21.25, y = 24$
- Ⓑ $x = 25, y = 41\frac{2}{3}$
- Ⓒ $x = 22, y = 31.67$
- Ⓓ $x = 25, y = 30$
- Ⓔ $x = 24, y = 28.3$

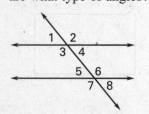

$(3y - 15)°$
$5(x - 4)°$
$3(x + 10)°$

13. *Multiple Choice*   In the diagram, $\angle 4$ and $\angle 5$ are what type of angles?

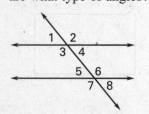

- Ⓐ   corresponding angles
- Ⓑ   alternate interior angles
- Ⓒ   alternate exterior angles
- Ⓓ   consecutive interior angles
- Ⓔ   consecutive exterior angles

14. *Multiple Choice*   Find the value of x when $a \parallel b$.

- Ⓐ   15
- Ⓑ   16
- Ⓒ   17
- Ⓓ   18
- Ⓔ   19

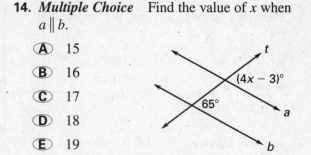

t
$(4x - 3)°$
$65°$
a
b

15. *Multiple Choice*   What value of a would make lines x and y parallel?

- Ⓐ   29
- Ⓑ   36
- Ⓒ   7
- Ⓓ   14
- Ⓔ   58

t
$5a°$ x
$145°$ y

16. *Quantitative Comparison*   **Choose the statement below that is true.**

- Ⓐ   The value in column A is greater.
- Ⓑ   The value in column B is greater.
- Ⓒ   The two values are equal.
- Ⓓ   The relationship cannot be determined from the given information.

Column A	Column B
Slope of the line $5x + 2y = 12$	Slope of the line perpendicular to $y = \frac{2}{3}x + 6$

17. *Multiple Choice*   Find the measure of $\angle 1$.

- Ⓐ $32°$
- Ⓑ $35°$
- Ⓒ $90°$
- Ⓓ $58°$
- Ⓔ $55°$

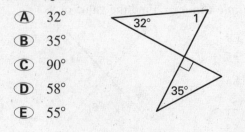

$32°$ 1
$35°$

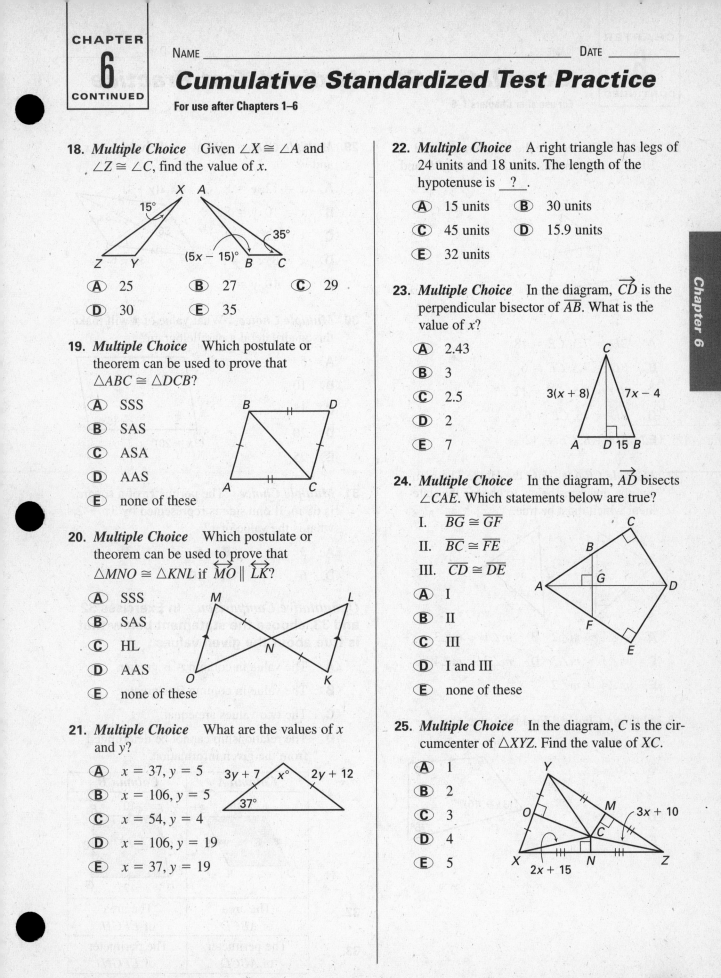

18. *Multiple Choice* Given $\angle X \cong \angle A$ and $\angle Z \cong \angle C$, find the value of x.

Ⓐ 25 Ⓑ 27 Ⓒ 29

Ⓓ 30 Ⓔ 35

19. *Multiple Choice* Which postulate or theorem can be used to prove that $\triangle ABC \cong \triangle DCB$?

Ⓐ SSS

Ⓑ SAS

Ⓒ ASA

Ⓓ AAS

Ⓔ none of these

20. *Multiple Choice* Which postulate or theorem can be used to prove that $\triangle MNO \cong \triangle KNL$ if $\overleftrightarrow{MO} \parallel \overleftrightarrow{LK}$?

Ⓐ SSS

Ⓑ SAS

Ⓒ HL

Ⓓ AAS

Ⓔ none of these

21. *Multiple Choice* What are the values of x and y?

Ⓐ $x = 37, y = 5$

Ⓑ $x = 106, y = 5$

Ⓒ $x = 54, y = 4$

Ⓓ $x = 106, y = 19$

Ⓔ $x = 37, y = 19$

22. *Multiple Choice* A right triangle has legs of 24 units and 18 units. The length of the hypotenuse is ___?___ .

Ⓐ 15 units Ⓑ 30 units

Ⓒ 45 units Ⓓ 15.9 units

Ⓔ 32 units

23. *Multiple Choice* In the diagram, $\overrightarrow{CD}$ is the perpendicular bisector of $\overline{AB}$. What is the value of x?

Ⓐ 2.43

Ⓑ 3

Ⓒ 2.5

Ⓓ 2

Ⓔ 7

24. *Multiple Choice* In the diagram, $\overrightarrow{AD}$ bisects $\angle CAE$. Which statements below are true?

I. $\overline{BG} \cong \overline{GF}$

II. $\overline{BC} \cong \overline{FE}$

III. $\overline{CD} \cong \overline{DE}$

Ⓐ I

Ⓑ II

Ⓒ III

Ⓓ I and III

Ⓔ none of these

25. *Multiple Choice* In the diagram, C is the circumcenter of $\triangle XYZ$. Find the value of XC.

Ⓐ 1

Ⓑ 2

Ⓒ 3

Ⓓ 4

Ⓔ 5

26. Multiple Choice In the diagram, $\overline{BD}$ and $\overline{BF}$ are midsegments of $\triangle ACE$. Find BD and CE.

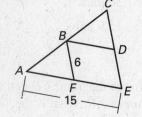

- (A) $BD = 7.5$, $CE = 18$
- (B) $BD = 7.5$, $CE = 6$
- (C) $BD = 7.5$, $CE = 12$
- (D) $BD = 15$, $CE = 6$
- (E) $BD = 8$, $CE = 12$

27. Multiple Choice Use the Hinge Theorem and the diagrams below to choose the statement which must be true.

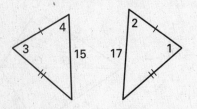

- (A) $m\angle 1 > m\angle 2$
- (B) $m\angle 1 < m\angle 3$
- (C) $m\angle 1 > m\angle 3$
- (D) $m\angle 2 < m\angle 4$
- (E) $m\angle 4 > m\angle 2$

28. Multiple Choice Find the value of x.

- (A) 15
- (B) 16
- (C) 18
- (D) 19
- (E) 21

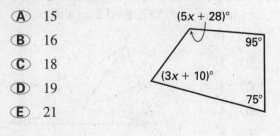

29. Multiple Choice What are the values of x and y?

- (A) $x = 12$, $y = 8$
- (B) $x = 10$, $y = 8$
- (C) $x = 12$, $y = 4$
- (D) $x = 8$, $y = 4$
- (E) $x = 10$, $y = 7$

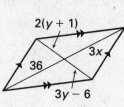

30. Multiple Choice What value of x will make the quadrilateral a parallelogram?

- (A) 5
- (B) 10
- (C) 15
- (D) 20
- (E) 25

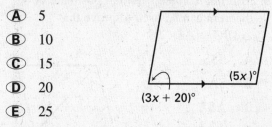

31. Multiple Choice The perimeter of a square is 68 m. If one side is represented by $3x + 2$, what is the value of x?

- (A) 3
- (B) 5
- (C) 4
- (D) 6
- (E) 10

Quantitative Comparison In Exercises 32 and 33, choose the statement below that is true about the given values.

- (A) The value in column A is greater.
- (B) The value in column B is greater.
- (C) The two values are equal.
- (D) The relationship cannot be determined from the given information.

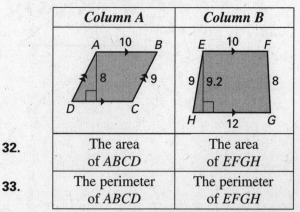

	Column A	Column B
32.	The area of ABCD	The area of EFGH
33.	The perimeter of ABCD	The perimeter of EFGH

NAME _____ DATE _____

Standardized Test Practice

For use with pages 396–402

TEST TAKING STRATEGY   **Sketch graphs or figures in your test booklet to help you solve the problems. Even though you must keep your answer sheet neat, you can make any kind of mark you want in your test booklet.**

1. **Multiple Choice**   Which of the statements below are true?

   I.   Rigid transformations are isometries.

   II. Three types of transformations are reflections, rotations, and transcriptions.

   III. Isometries preserve distances between points.

   (A) I   (B) I and II

   (C) II and III   (D) I and III

   (E) None of these

2. **Multiple Choice**   Which of the following is *not* an isometry?

   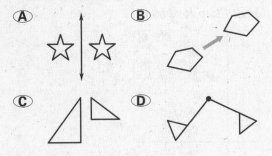

   (E) None of these

3. **Multiple Choice**   Name the preimage of $\overline{MN}$.

   (A) $\overline{AB}$
   (B) $\overline{BC}$
   (C) $\overline{CD}$
   (D) $\overline{DF}$
   (E) $\overline{FA}$

   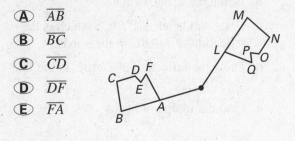

4. **Multiple Choice**   Name the type of transformation and the coordinates corresponding to point A'.

   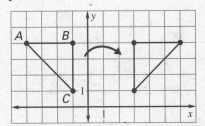

   (A) reflection in line $x = 1$, $(3, 4)$

   (B) reflection in line $x = 0$, $(3, 4)$

   (C) rotation about $(1, 0)$, $(6, 4)$

   (D) reflection in line $x = 1$, $(6, 4)$

   (E) translation in line $x = 1$, $(6, 4)$

Quantitative Comparison   **In Exercises 5 and 6, use the isometry of the kite to find the value of the variables. Choose the statement below that is true about the values.**

   (A) The value in column A is greater.

   (B) The value in column B is greater.

   (C) The two values are equal.

   (D) The relationship cannot be determined from the given information.

   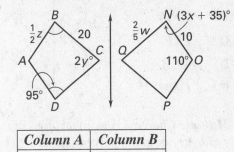

	Column A	Column B
5.	x	y
6.	w	z

Standardized Test Practice

For use with pages 404–410

TEST TAKING STRATEGY **Work as quickly as you can through the easier sections, but avoid making careless errors on easy questions.**

1. *Multiple Choice* Which choice below is a reflection of the figure in line *h*?

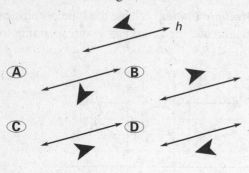

   (E) None of these

2. *Multiple Choice* If $A(3, -2)$ is reflected in the line $x = 3$, then the coordinates of A' are ___?___ .

   (A) $(0, -2)$ (B) $(3, -2)$ (C) $(3, 1)$

   (D) $(-3, 2)$ (E) $(0, 1)$

3. *Multiple Choice* If $B(-2, -1)$ is reflected in the line $y = 3$, then the coordinates of B' are ___?___ .

   (A) $(4, 5)$ (B) $(-2, 5)$

   (C) $(-2, -1)$ (D) $(8, 5)$

   (E) $(-2, 7)$

4. *Multiple Choice* Use the diagram below to complete the statement: $\angle GHI \rightarrow$ ___?___ .

   (A) $\angle NOP$

   (B) $\angle KPO$

   (C) $\angle LKP$

   (D) $\angle KLM$

   (E) $\angle ONM$

   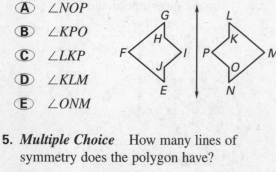

5. *Multiple Choice* How many lines of symmetry does the polygon have?

   (A) 0 (B) 1

   (C) 2 (D) 3

   (E) 4

   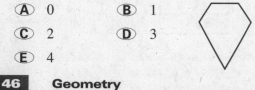

6. *Multiple Choice* Given $A(3, -4)$ and $B(6, -2)$, find point C on the *x*-axis so that $AC + BC$ is a minimum.

   (A) $(0, 4)$ (B) $(0, 5)$ (C) $(3, 0)$

   (D) $(4, 0)$ (E) $(5, 0)$

7. *Multiple Choice* Given that the diagram shows a reflection in line *m*, find the values of *x* and *y*.

   (A) $x = 10, y = \frac{3}{2}$

   (B) $x = 10, y = 4$

   (C) $x = \frac{5}{2}, y = \frac{3}{2}$

   (D) $x = \frac{5}{2}, y = 4$

   (E) $x = 6, y = \frac{13}{8}$

   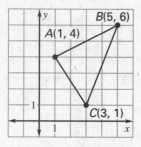

8. *Multi-Step Problem*

   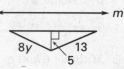

   a. Draw and label $\triangle A'B'C'$, which is the reflection of $\triangle ABC$ in the *x*-axis.

   b. Name the image of $\overline{AB}$.

   c. Draw and label $\triangle A''B''C''$, which is the reflection of $\triangle ABC$ in the *y*-axis.

   d. Draw the reflection of $\triangle ABC$ in the line $x = 2$.

   e. Find the midpoint of $\overline{AA'}$.

Chapter 7

NAME _____ DATE _____

Standardized Test Practice

For use with pages 412–420

TEST TAKING STRATEGY   **Make sure that you are familiar with the directions before taking a standardized test.**

1. *Multiple Choice*   Use the figure below to determine which segment represents a 90° clockwise rotation of $\overline{AB}$ about *P*.

   Ⓐ $\overline{BC}$
   Ⓑ $\overline{CD}$
   Ⓒ $\overline{DE}$
   Ⓓ $\overline{AH}$
   Ⓔ $\overline{HG}$

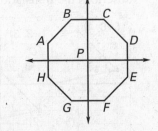

2. *Multiple Choice*   Which description of a rotation would map the figure below onto itself?

   Ⓐ clockwise 45°
   Ⓑ clockwise 90°
   Ⓒ clockwise 180°
   Ⓓ counterclockwise 45°
   Ⓔ none of these

Multiple Choice   Use the figure below for Exercises 3 and 4. State the segment or triangle that represents the image.

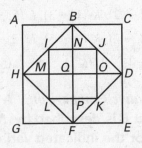

3. A 90° clockwise rotation of $\overline{HI}$ about *Q*.

   Ⓐ $\overline{LF}$ Ⓑ $\overline{HL}$ Ⓒ $\overline{KO}$
   Ⓓ $\overline{BJ}$ Ⓔ $\overline{JD}$

4. A 90° counterclockwise rotation of $\overline{QO}$ about *P*.

   Ⓐ $\overline{QN}$ Ⓑ $\overline{MQ}$ Ⓒ $\overline{LP}$
   Ⓓ $\overline{OK}$ Ⓔ $\overline{LM}$

5. *Multiple Choice*   Find the angle of rotation that maps $\triangle ABC$ onto $\triangle A''B''C''$.

   Ⓐ 60°
   Ⓑ 30°
   Ⓒ 120°
   Ⓓ 180°
   Ⓔ None of these

6. *Multiple Choice* $\triangle ABC$ has vertices $A(-2, 1)$, $B(3, 2)$ and $C(5, -1)$. What are the coordinates of the vertices of $\triangle A'B'C'$ after a rotation of 180° clockwise about the origin?

   Ⓐ $A'(2, -1)$, $B'(-3, -2)$, $C'(-5, 1)$
   Ⓑ $A'(-2, -1)$, $B'(-3, -2)$, $C'(-5, -1)$
   Ⓒ $A'(-2, -1)$, $B'(-3, -2)$, $C'(-5, 1)$
   Ⓓ $A'(2, 1)$, $B'(3, 2)$, $C'(5, 1)$
   Ⓔ $A'(2, -1)$, $B'(3, 2)$, $C'(-5, 1)$

7. *Quantitative Comparison*   **Use the diagram below to find the value of each variable in the rotation of the polygon about point *P*. Choose the statement below that is true about the values.**

   Ⓐ The value in column A is greater.
   Ⓑ The value in column B is greater.
   Ⓒ The two values are equal.
   Ⓓ The relationship cannot be determined from the given information.

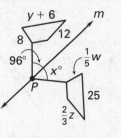

Column A	Column B
y	z

TEST TAKING STRATEGY   **If you find yourself spending too much time on one test question and getting frustrated, move on to the next question. You can revisit a difficult problem later with a fresh perspective.**

1. Multiple Choice   The translation "5 units to the left and 3 units up" in coordinate notation would be ___?___.

(A) $(x, y) \rightarrow (x + 5, y + 3)$

(B) $(x, y) \rightarrow (x + 5, y - 3)$

(C) $(x, y) \rightarrow (x - 5, y + 3)$

(D) $(x, y) \rightarrow (x + 3, y - 5)$

(E) $(x, y) \rightarrow (x - 3, y + 5)$

2. Multiple Choice   Choose the notation below that describes the translation.

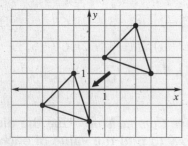

(A) $(x, y) \rightarrow (x - 3, y + 4)$

(B) $(x, y) \rightarrow (x - 3, y - 4)$

(C) $(x, y) \rightarrow (x - 4, y + 3)$

(D) $(x, y) \rightarrow (x - 4, y - 3)$

(E) $(x, y) \rightarrow (x + 4, y + 3)$

3. Multiple Choice   Choose the correct name and component form of the vector shown.

(A) $\overrightarrow{JH}, \langle 3, 4 \rangle$

(B) $\overrightarrow{JH}, \langle -3, -4 \rangle$

(C) $\overrightarrow{JH}, \langle -4, -3 \rangle$

(D) $\overrightarrow{HJ}, \langle 3, 4 \rangle$

(E) $\overrightarrow{HJ}, \langle -3, -4 \rangle$

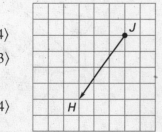

4. Multiple Choice   Name the vector that describes the translation.

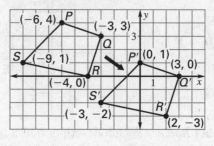

(A) $\langle -6, -3 \rangle$ (B) $\langle 6, 3 \rangle$

(C) $\langle -3, 6 \rangle$ (D) $\langle 3, -6 \rangle$

(E) $\langle 6, -3 \rangle$

5. Multiple Choice   The coordinates of $\triangle JKL$ are $J(-1, 2)$, $K(-2, -1)$, and $L(2, 1)$. The component form of $\overrightarrow{MN}$ is $\langle 3, -4 \rangle$. What are the coordinates of $\triangle J'K'L'$ after the translation using $\overrightarrow{MN}$?

(A) $J'(-4, -2), K'(1, -3), L'(5, -5)$

(B) $J'(2, -2), K'(1, -3), L'(5, -3)$

(C) $J'(2, -2), K'(1, -3), L'(5, -5)$

(D) $J'(2, -2), K'(1, -5), L'(5, -3)$

(E) $J'(-4, -2), K'(1, -5), L'(5, -3)$

6. Quantitative Comparison   **A translation of A and B is described by $\overrightarrow{NM} = \langle 7, 2 \rangle$. Solve for the indicated variables. Choose the statement below that is true about the values of the variables.**

(A) The value in column A is greater.

(B) The value in column B is greater.

(C) The two values are equal.

(D) The relationship cannot be determined from the given information.

Column A	Column B
$A(-3, y)$, $A'(4, 4)$	$B(x, 5)$, $B'(10, 7)$

TEST TAKING STRATEGY **One of the best ways to prepare for the SAT is to keep up with your regular studies and do your homework.**

1. *Multiple Choice* Which two transformations were performed to obtain $\overline{A''B''}$ in the diagram?

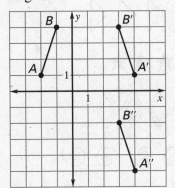

- (A) Rotate about the origin, then reflect in $x = y$.
- (B) Reflect in the x-axis, then translate parallel to x-axis.
- (C) Reflect in the line $x = 1$, then translate parallel to $x = 1$.
- (D) Reflect in the line $y = 1$, then translate parallel to $y = -1$.
- (E) Translate parallel to $x = 1$, then reflect in line $x = 1$.

2. *Quantitative Comparison* **Use the composition to locate points A'' and B''. Choose the statement below that is true about the given lengths.**

- (A) The value in column A is greater.
- (B) The value in column B is greater.
- (C) The two values are equal.
- (D) The relationship cannot be determined from the given information.

Given: $A(-4, 0)$, $B(-2, -1)$

Reflection: in $x = 1$

Rotation: 90° counterclockwise about (2, 1)

Column A	Column B
length of $\overline{AA''}$	length of $\overline{BB''}$

3. *Multiple Choice* Using the composition below, what are the coordinates of the endpoints of $\overline{A''B''}$?

Given: $A(1, 3)$, $B(2, 5)$

Rotation: 90° counterclockwise about (2, 1)

Reflection: in $y = x$

- (A) $A''(0, 0)$, $B''(1, -2)$
- (B) $A''(-2, 1)$, $B''(-4, 0)$
- (C) $A''(2, 1)$, $B''(-4, 0)$
- (D) $A''(2, 1)$, $B''(4, 0)$
- (E) $A''(0, 0)$, $B''(-1, 2)$

4. *Multiple Choice* Translation 1 maps A to A'. Translation 2 maps A' to A''. What translation below maps A to A''?

Translation 1: $(x, y) \rightarrow (x - 2, y + 6)$
Translation 2: $(x, y) \rightarrow (x + 7, y - 6)$

- (A) $(x, y) \rightarrow (x - 5, y + 6)$
- (B) $(x, y) \rightarrow (x + 5, y)$
- (C) $(x, y) \rightarrow (x + 5, y + 12)$
- (D) $(x, y) \rightarrow (x + 9, y - 12)$
- (E) $(x, y) \rightarrow (x - 9, y)$

5. *Multiple Choice* Using the composition below, what are the coordinates of the endpoints of $\overline{C''D''}$?

Given: $C(-2, 3)$, $D(3, 4)$

Rotation: 90° clockwise about origin

Reflection: in $x = 1$

- (A) $C''(5, -2)$, $D''(6, 3)$
- (B) $C''(1, 2)$, $D''(2, 3)$
- (C) $C''(-5, -2)$, $D''(-6, 3)$
- (D) $C''(-1, 2)$, $D''(-2, -3)$
- (E) $C''(-1, 2)$, $D''(2, 3)$

TEST TAKING STRATEGY   **Do not put added pressure on yourself to do well. If you are not satisfied with your SAT score, you can take it again.**

1. *Multiple Choice*   A frieze pattern is a pattern that extends to the left and right in such a way that the pattern can be mapped onto itself by a

   Ⓐ   vertical translation.

   Ⓑ   vertical reflection.

   Ⓒ   horizontal translation.

   Ⓓ   horizontal reflection.

   Ⓔ   horizontal glide reflection.

In Exercises 2–7, use these classifications.

   T   translation
   R   180° rotation
   H   horizontal reflection
   V   vertical reflection
   G   horizontal glide reflection

2. *Multiple Choice*   Name the isometries that map the frieze pattern onto itself.

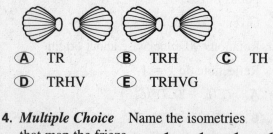

   Ⓐ   T   Ⓑ   TR   Ⓒ   TV

   Ⓓ   TH   Ⓔ   TG

3. *Multiple Choice*   Name the isometries that map the frieze pattern onto itself.

   Ⓐ   TR   Ⓑ   TRH   Ⓒ   TH

   Ⓓ   TRHV   Ⓔ   TRHVG

4. *Multiple Choice*   Name the isometries that map the frieze pattern onto itself.

   Ⓐ   TH

   Ⓑ   TR   Ⓒ   THV

   Ⓓ   TV   Ⓔ   THG

5. *Multiple Choice*   Which design below is a frieze pattern with a classification of TV?

   Ⓐ

   Ⓑ

   Ⓒ

   Ⓓ

   Ⓔ

6. *Multiple Choice*   Which design below is a frieze pattern with a classification of TRVG?

   Ⓐ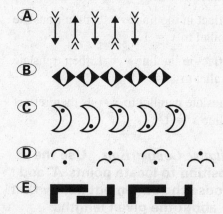

   Ⓑ

   Ⓒ

   Ⓓ

   Ⓔ

7. *Multi-Step Problem*   Use the pattern below to create a frieze pattern with the given classifications.

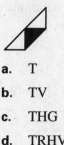

   a.   T

   b.   TV

   c.   THG

   d.   TRHVG

Geometry
Standardized Test Practice Workbook

Standardized Test Practice

For use with pages 457–464

TEST TAKING STRATEGY Work as quickly as you can through the easier sections, but avoid making careless errors on easy questions.

1. Multiple Choice Simplify $\dfrac{3 \text{ ft}}{18 \text{ in.}}$.

  A $\frac{1}{2}$ **B** 2   **C** $\frac{1}{6}$

  D 6   **E** $\frac{15}{8}$

2. Multiple Choice Simplify $\dfrac{5 \text{ m}}{125 \text{ cm}}$.

  A 25   **B** 0.04   **C** 4

  D 0.25   **E** 40

3. Multiple Choice The perimeter of rectangle *ABCD* is 72. The ratio of the lengths of the sides is 1:2. What are the lengths of the sides?

  A 12 and 18   **B** 12 and 24

  C 4.5 and 9   **D** 6 and 12

  E 9 and 18

4. Multiple Choice The perimeter of △*HIJ* is 36. The extended ratio of the sides is 2:3:7. Find the lengths of the sides.

  A 3, 4, 9   **B** 4, 6, 14

  C 8, 12, 28   **D** 6, 9, 21

  E 2, 3, 7

5. Multiple Choice Solve $\dfrac{5}{x+7} = \dfrac{3}{x+2}$.

  A 2   **B** 3   **C** $\frac{3}{2}$

  D $\frac{5}{2}$ **E** $\frac{11}{2}$

6. Multiple Choice Which ratio describes the simplified width to length ratio of *ABCD*?

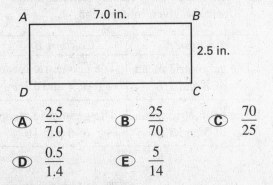

  A $\frac{2.5}{7.0}$ **B** $\frac{25}{70}$ **C** $\frac{70}{25}$

  D $\frac{0.5}{1.4}$ **E** $\frac{5}{14}$

7. Multiple Choice The ratio of side lengths of △*ABC* to △*DEF* is 3:1. Find the lengths of $\overline{EF}$ and $\overline{AC}$.

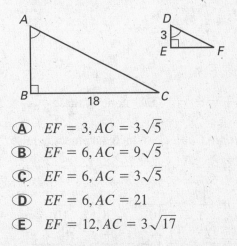

  A $EF = 3, AC = 3\sqrt{5}$

  B $EF = 6, AC = 9\sqrt{5}$

  C $EF = 6, AC = 3\sqrt{5}$

  D $EF = 6, AC = 21$

  E $EF = 12, AC = 3\sqrt{17}$

Quantitative Comparison For Exercises 8 and 9, use the number line below to find the ratio of the distances. Choose the statement below that is true about the given values.

  A The value in column A is greater.

  B The value in column B is greater.

  C The values are equal.

  D The relationship cannot be determined from the given information.

```
      A   B        C   D   E  F
   ┼──●───●───┼───┼───●───●───●──●──┼──►
  -4  -2   0   2   4   6   8  10
```

	Column A	Column B
8.	$\dfrac{EF}{AB}$	$\dfrac{CD}{CE}$
9.	$\dfrac{AC}{BE}$	$\dfrac{DF}{BD}$

Chapter 8

Standardized Test Practice

For use with pages 465–471

TEST TAKING STRATEGY   **Do not panic if you run out of time before answering all of the questions. You can still receive a high test score without answering every question.**

1. *Multiple Choice*   Which choice below completes the sentence to make a true statement?

   "If $\dfrac{3}{x} = \dfrac{7}{y}$, then ___?___."

   (A) $\dfrac{3}{x} = \dfrac{y}{7}$ (B) $\dfrac{3}{7} = \dfrac{y}{x}$ (C) $\dfrac{x}{3} = \dfrac{7}{y}$

   (D) $\dfrac{3}{7} = \dfrac{x}{y}$ (E)   none of these

2. *Multiple Choice*   Which statement is false?

   (A) If $\dfrac{5}{x} = \dfrac{y}{3}$, then $\dfrac{5+x}{x} = \dfrac{y+3}{3}$.

   (B) If $\dfrac{17}{x+2} = \dfrac{8}{10}$, then $\dfrac{17}{8} = \dfrac{x+2}{10}$.

   (C) If $\dfrac{15}{x} = \dfrac{17}{y}$, then $\dfrac{15+y}{x} = \dfrac{17+x}{y}$.

   (D) If $\dfrac{6+7}{7} = \dfrac{5+n}{n}$, then $\dfrac{6}{7} = \dfrac{5}{n}$.

   (E) If $\dfrac{9}{7} = \dfrac{x}{12}$, then $\dfrac{12}{x} = \dfrac{7}{9}$.

3. *Multiple Choice*   In the diagram, $\dfrac{AB}{BD} = \dfrac{AC}{CE}$.
   Find the length of $\overline{AE}$.

   (A) 7.5

   (B) 15

   (C) 17.5

   (D) $13\frac{1}{3}$

   (E) $28\frac{1}{3}$

4. *Multiple Choice*   In the diagram, $\dfrac{UV}{UZ} = \dfrac{WX}{WY}$.
   Find the length of $\overline{WX}$.

   (A) $2\frac{1}{3}$

   (B) 3.5

   (C) 10.5

   (D) $4\frac{2}{3}$

   (E) $11\frac{2}{3}$

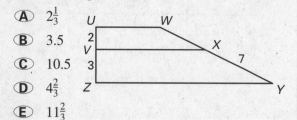

5. *Multiple Choice*   The geometric mean of x and 5 is 15. Find the value of x.

   (A) 3   (B) 10   (C) 15

   (D) $5\sqrt{3}$ (E) 45

6. *Multiple Choice*   There are 36 students in a gym class. If $\frac{1}{4}$ of the students are freshmen and $\frac{2}{3}$ of the remaining students are seniors, how many seniors are in the class?

   (A) 6   (B) 12   (C) 15

   (D) 18   (E) 24

7. *Multiple Choice*   The points $(-3, 1)$, $(3, 3)$, and $(x, 5)$ are collinear. Find the value of x by setting up and solving a proportion.

   (A) 1   (B) 2   (C) 9

   (D) 5   (E) 4

8. *Multiple Choice*   A model truck is 13.5 inches long and 7.5 inches wide. The original truck was 12 feet long. How wide was it?

   (A) $6\frac{2}{3}$ ft   (B) 7.5 ft   (C) $5\frac{4}{5}$ ft

   (D) 8.4 ft   (E) 21.6 ft

Quantitative Comparison   **In Exercises 9 and 10, choose the statement below that is true about the given value.**

   (A) The value in column A is greater.

   (B) The value in column B is greater.

   (C) The two values are equal.

   (D) The relationship cannot be determined from the given information.

	Column A	Column B
9.	The geometric mean of 8 and 16	The geometric mean of 7 and 19
10.	The geometric mean of 5 and 12	The geometric mean of 6 and 10

Geometry
Standardized Test Practice Workbook

NAME _____ DATE _____

Standardized Test Practice

TEST TAKING STRATEGY **Always look for shortcuts that will allow you to work through a problem more quickly.**

1. *Multiple Choice*   Hexagons *ABCDEF* and *MNOPQR* are similar. Which statement of proportionality is *not* true?

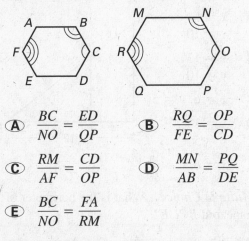

Ⓐ $\dfrac{BC}{NO} = \dfrac{ED}{QP}$ Ⓑ $\dfrac{RQ}{FE} = \dfrac{OP}{CD}$

Ⓒ $\dfrac{RM}{AF} = \dfrac{CD}{OP}$ Ⓓ $\dfrac{MN}{AB} = \dfrac{PQ}{DE}$

Ⓔ $\dfrac{BC}{NO} = \dfrac{FA}{RM}$

2. *Multiple Choice*   The two trapezoids shown are similar. What are the values of *x* and *y*?

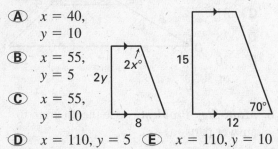

Ⓐ $x = 40,$ $y = 10$

Ⓑ $x = 55,$ $y = 5$

Ⓒ $x = 55,$ $y = 10$

Ⓓ $x = 110, y = 5$ Ⓔ $x = 110, y = 10$

3. *Multiple Choice*   Find the scale factor of *MNOP* to *QRST*, given that *MNOP* ~ *QRST*.

Ⓐ 1:5

Ⓑ 3:5

Ⓒ 2:5

Ⓓ 5:2

Ⓔ 5:3

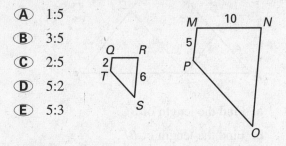

4. *Multiple Choice*   The ratio of the perimeters of △*ABC* to △*KLM* is 3:5. Which ratio could *not* be a ratio of two corresponding sides?

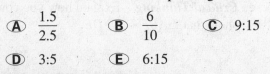

Ⓐ $\dfrac{1.5}{2.5}$ Ⓑ $\dfrac{6}{10}$ Ⓒ 9:15

Ⓓ 3:5   Ⓔ 6:15

5. *Multiple Choice*   *ABCD* ~ *EFGH*. The perimeter of *ABCD* is 18. What is the length of $\overline{BC}$?

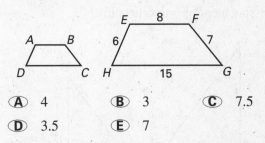

Ⓐ 4   Ⓑ 3   Ⓒ 7.5

Ⓓ 3.5   Ⓔ 7

6. *Multiple Choice*   The ratio of one side of *ABCD* to the corresponding side of *EFGH* is 1.5 to 4. The perimeter of *EFGH* is 38 inches. Find the perimeter of *ABCD*.

Ⓐ 14.25 in.   Ⓑ 28.5 in.   Ⓒ $6\frac{1}{3}$ in.

Ⓓ $101\frac{1}{3}$ in.   Ⓔ $50\frac{2}{3}$ in.

Quantitative Comparison   **In Exercises 7 and 8, use the diagram to choose the statement that is true given that** ***ABCDE* ~ *LMNOP*.**

Ⓐ   The value in column A is greater.

Ⓑ   The value in column B is greater.

Ⓒ   The two values are equal.

Ⓓ   The relationship cannot be determined from the given information.

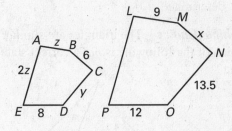

	Column A	Column B
7.	*x*	*y*
8.	*AE* + *AB*	*LP*

Standardized Test Practice

For use with pages 480–487

TEST TAKING STRATEGY   **When checking your work, try to use a method other than the one you originally used to get your answer. If you use the same method, you may make the same mistake twice.**

1. *Multiple Choice* The triangles below are similar. Which choice below is the correct statement of proportionality?

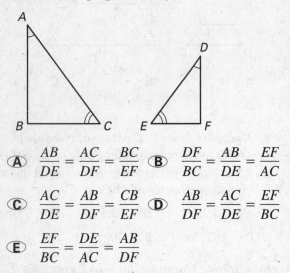

Ⓐ $\dfrac{AB}{DE} = \dfrac{AC}{DF} = \dfrac{BC}{EF}$ Ⓑ $\dfrac{DF}{BC} = \dfrac{AB}{DE} = \dfrac{EF}{AC}$

Ⓒ $\dfrac{AC}{DE} = \dfrac{AB}{DF} = \dfrac{CB}{EF}$ Ⓓ $\dfrac{AB}{DF} = \dfrac{AC}{DE} = \dfrac{EF}{BC}$

Ⓔ $\dfrac{EF}{BC} = \dfrac{DE}{AC} = \dfrac{AB}{DF}$

2. *Multiple Choice* Which angle is congruent to ∠M in the similar triangles below?

Ⓐ ∠N
Ⓑ ∠Q
Ⓒ ∠QOP
Ⓓ ∠P
Ⓔ cannot be determined

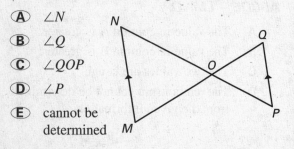

3. *Multiple Choice* The triangles are similar. Which of the following is *not* a correct statement?

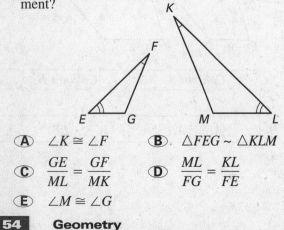

Ⓐ ∠K ≅ ∠F   Ⓑ △FEG ~ △KLM

Ⓒ $\dfrac{GE}{ML} = \dfrac{GF}{MK}$ Ⓓ $\dfrac{ML}{FG} = \dfrac{KL}{FE}$

Ⓔ ∠M ≅ ∠G

4. *Multiple Choice* △ABC ~ △DBE. Find the values of x and y.

Ⓐ x = 6, y = 10

Ⓑ x = 13½, y = 10

Ⓒ x = 6, y = 5

Ⓓ x = 13½, y = 5

Ⓔ x = 6, y = $\frac{10}{3}$

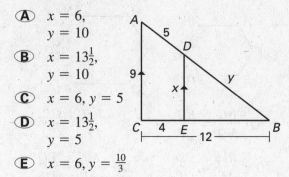

5. *Multiple Choice* What is the perimeter of trapezoid *BCDE*?

Ⓐ 26
Ⓑ 28
Ⓒ 31
Ⓓ 38
Ⓔ 30 or 30.1

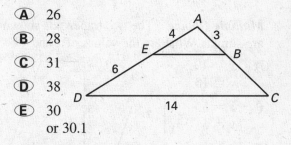

6. *Multi-Step Problem* Use the diagram to answer parts (a)–(e).

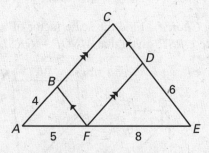

a. Find the length of $\overline{BC}$.

b. Find the length of $\overline{BF}$.

c. What is the scale factor of △ABF to △ACE?

d. Find the perimeter of ▱BCDF.

e. *Critical Thinking* Explain how you could show that △ABF ~ △FDE.

NAME _____ DATE _____

Standardized Test Practice

For use with pages 488–496

TEST TAKING STRATEGY   Sketch graphs or figures in your test booklet to help you solve the problems. Even though you must keep your answer sheet neat, you can make any kind of mark you want in your test booklet.

1. **Multiple Choice**   Use the diagram below to determine which statement(s) are true.

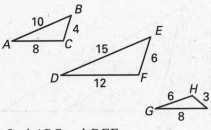

   I. △ABC ~ △DEF
  II. △ABC ~ △GHI
 III. △DEF ~ △GHI

  Ⓐ   I   Ⓑ   II   Ⓒ   III
  Ⓓ   I and III   Ⓔ   none of these

2. **Multiple Choice**   What is the scale factor for the triangles below?

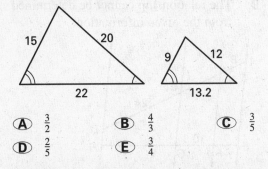

  Ⓐ $\frac{3}{2}$ Ⓑ $\frac{4}{3}$ Ⓒ $\frac{3}{5}$
  Ⓓ $\frac{2}{5}$ Ⓔ $\frac{3}{4}$

3. **Multiple Choice**   Which similarity statement and postulate or theorem correctly identifies the triangles' relationship?

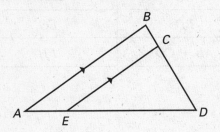

  Ⓐ   △ABD ~ △ECD by SSS Similarity Thm.
  Ⓑ   △ABD ~ △ECD by SAS Similarity Thm.

  Ⓒ   △ABD ~ △DEC by SSS Similarity Thm.
  Ⓓ   △ABD ~ △ECD by AA Similarity Post.
  Ⓔ   △ABD ~ △DEC by AA Similarity Post.

4. **Multiple Choice**   Which similarity statement and postulate or theorem correctly identifies the triangles' relationship?

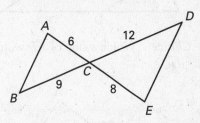

  Ⓐ   △ABC ~ △CDE by SSS Similarity Thm.
  Ⓑ   △ABC ~ △CDE by SAS Similarity Thm.
  Ⓒ   △ABC ~ △EDC by SSS Similarity Thm.
  Ⓓ   △ABC ~ △EDC by AA Similarity Post.
  Ⓔ   △ABC ~ △EDC by SAS Similarity Thm.

5. **Multiple Choice**   Find the distance labeled x in the diagram.

  Ⓐ   32.5 ft
  Ⓑ   42.5 ft
  Ⓒ   35 ft
  Ⓓ   48.2 ft
  Ⓔ   43.5 ft

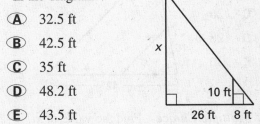

6. **Multiple Choice**   Solve for x.

  Ⓐ   18.75
  Ⓑ   17.2
  Ⓒ   18
  Ⓓ   19
  Ⓔ   12.5

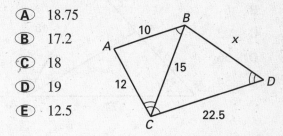

Standardized Test Practice

For use with pages 498–505

TEST TAKING STRATEGY It is important to remember that your SAT score will not solely determine your acceptance into a college or university. Do not put added pressure on yourself to do well. If you are not satisfied with your SAT score, remember that you can take it again.

1. Multiple Choice What is the length of $\overline{OP}$?

Ⓐ 1.5

Ⓑ $10\frac{2}{3}$

Ⓒ 5

Ⓓ 6

Ⓔ $7\frac{1}{3}$

2. Multiple Choice Which value of AB would make $\overline{EB} \parallel \overline{DC}$?

Ⓐ 4

Ⓑ 8

Ⓒ 18

Ⓓ 28

Ⓔ 36

3. Multiple Choice Find the value of x.

Ⓐ 22

Ⓑ 24

Ⓒ 26

Ⓓ 28

Ⓔ 30

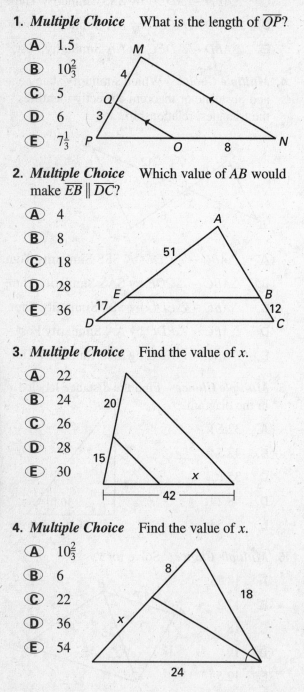

4. Multiple Choice Find the value of x.

Ⓐ $10\frac{2}{3}$

Ⓑ 6

Ⓒ 22

Ⓓ 36

Ⓔ 54

5. Multiple Choice Find the value of y.

Ⓐ 16

Ⓑ 36

Ⓒ 40

Ⓓ 54

Ⓔ 62

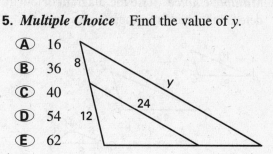

Quantitative Comparison In Exercises 6–8, use the diagram below to solve for the indicated values. Choose the statement that is true about the given values.

Ⓐ The value in column A is greater.

Ⓑ The value in column B is greater.

Ⓒ The two values are equal.

Ⓓ The relationship cannot be determined from the given information.

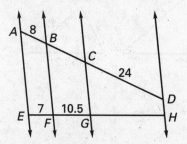

	Column A	Column B
6.	BC	GH
7.	BD	EG
8.	$AB + CD$	FH

Chapter 8

NAME _____ DATE _____

Standardized Test Practice

For use with pages 506–513

TEST TAKING STRATEGY **Avoid spending too much time on one question. Skip questions that are too difficult for you, and spend no more than a few minutes on each question.**

1. *Multiple Choice* Which statements below are true?

I. A dilation with a scale factor of $\frac{3}{2}$ is an enlargement, 50% bigger.

II. A dilation with a scale factor of $\frac{2}{3}$ is an enlargement, 66% bigger.

III. A dilation with scale factor k is a reduction if $-1 < k < 1$.

(A) I   (B) II   (C) III

(D) I and II   (E) II and III

2. *Multiple Choice* Which choice below correctly identifies the dilation and scale factor?

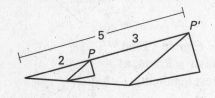

(A) reduction; $k = \frac{2}{5}$

(B) reduction; $k = \frac{3}{5}$

(C) enlargement; $k = \frac{2}{5}$

(D) enlargement; $k = \frac{3}{5}$

(E) enlargement; $k = \frac{5}{2}$

3. *Multiple Choice* Which choice below correctly identifies the dilation and scale factor?

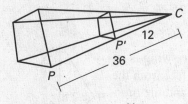

(A) reduction; $k = \frac{14}{36}$

(B) reduction; $k = \frac{36}{12}$

(C) reduction; $k = \frac{12}{36}$

(D) enlargement; $k = \frac{36}{12}$

(E) enlargement; $k = \frac{12}{36}$

4. *Multiple Choice* Find the values of x and y.

(A) $x = \frac{2}{3}$, $y = 8$

(B) $x = 6$, $y = 8$

(C) $x = 6$, $y = 12$

(D) $x = 6, y = 4$

(E) $x = 24, y = 4$

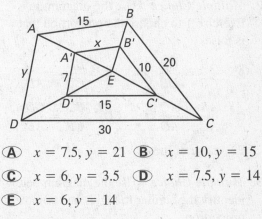

5. *Multiple Choice* The dilation has center E. Find the values of x and y.

(A) $x = 7.5, y = 21$ (B) $x = 10, y = 15$

(C) $x = 6, y = 3.5$ (D) $x = 7.5, y = 14$

(E) $x = 6, y = 14$

6. *Multi-Step Problem*

a. On a coordinate plane, draw $\triangle ABC$ with vertices $A(1, 5)$, $B(3, 6)$, and $C(3, 3)$.

b. Draw a dilation of $\triangle ABC$. Use the origin as center and a scale factor of 2 to draw $\triangle A'B'C'$.

c. Find the length of $\overline{B'C'}$.

d. Draw a dilation of $\triangle ABC$. Use the origin as center and a scale factor of $\frac{1}{2}$ to draw $\triangle A''B''C''$.

e. Find the length of $\overline{A''C''}$.

f. What scale factor could you use to go from $\triangle A''B''C''$ to $\triangle A'B'C'$?

NAME _____ DATE _____

Standardized Test Practice

For use with pages 527–534

TEST TAKING STRATEGY Read each test question carefully. Always look for shortcuts that will allow you to work through a problem more quickly.

1. Multiple Choice Use the diagram at the right to choose the correct similarity statement for the three triangles.

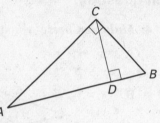

- Ⓐ $\triangle ABC \sim \triangle CDB \sim \triangle ACD$
- Ⓑ $\triangle ABC \sim \triangle CBD \sim \triangle ADC$
- Ⓒ $\triangle ABC \sim \triangle CBD \sim \triangle ACD$
- Ⓓ $\triangle ABC \sim \triangle CDB \sim \triangle ADC$
- Ⓔ $\triangle ABC \sim \triangle BCD \sim \triangle ADC$

2. Multiple Choice Use the diagram in Exercise 1 to choose the proportion that is false.

- Ⓐ $\dfrac{AB}{CB} = \dfrac{CB}{DB}$
- Ⓑ $\dfrac{BD}{CD} = \dfrac{CD}{AD}$
- Ⓒ $\dfrac{AB}{AC} = \dfrac{AC}{AD}$
- Ⓓ $\dfrac{BD}{CB} = \dfrac{CD}{AB}$
- Ⓔ none of these

3. Multiple Choice Use the diagram below to identify the similar triangles and complete the proportion.

$\dfrac{CA}{BA} = \dfrac{BA}{?}$

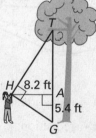

- Ⓐ AC
- Ⓑ BD
- Ⓒ DC
- Ⓓ BC
- Ⓔ DA

4. Multiple Choice Use the diagram below to find the value of h. Round to the nearest hundredth, if necessary.

- Ⓐ 9.60
- Ⓑ 9.50
- Ⓒ 8.70
- Ⓓ 10.23
- Ⓔ 9.25

5. Multiple Choice Find the value of y. Round to the nearest hundredth.

- Ⓐ 3.20
- Ⓑ 5.29
- Ⓒ 2.55
- Ⓓ 4.45
- Ⓔ 1.32

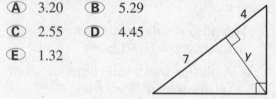

6. Multiple Choice Find the value of x. Round to the nearest hundredth.

- Ⓐ 10.2
- Ⓑ 3.08
- Ⓒ 8.06
- Ⓓ 5
- Ⓔ 8.13

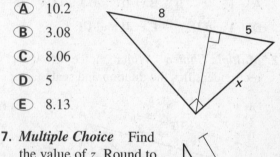

7. Multiple Choice Find the value of z. Round to the nearest hundredth.

- Ⓐ 42.68
- Ⓑ 20.49
- Ⓒ 64.29
- Ⓓ 56.28
- Ⓔ 62.30

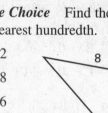

8. Multi-Step Problem You want to hang a tire swing from a tree in your backyard. The branch is horizontal to the ground. The diagram shows the vertical distance from your eye to the ground, and from you to the swing.

a. What is HG?

b. What is TG?

c. If the tire swing is to hang $2\frac{1}{2}$ feet from the ground, and the tire has a diameter of 3 feet, approximately how much rope is needed to hang the swing?

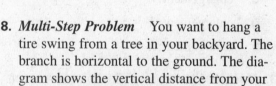

d. Write a similarity statement for the three triangles.

Standardized Test Practice

For use with pages 535–541

TEST TAKING STRATEGY   **When checking your work, try to use a method other than the one you originally used to get your answer. If you use the same method, you may make the same mistake twice.**

1. *Multiple Choice*   Which equations below are true about $\triangle ABC$?

   I. $a = \sqrt{c^2 - b^2}$

   II. $c = \sqrt{a^2 + b^2}$

   III. $b = c - a$

   (A) I   (B) II   (C) III

   (D) I and II   (E) all of these

2. *Multiple Choice*   Find the value of x. Round to the nearest tenth, if necessary.

   (A) 25 in.

   (B) 26.4 in.

   (C) 14 in.

   (D) 13.6 in.

   (E) 14.2 in.

3. *Multiple Choice*   Find the value of y. Round to the nearest hundredth, if necessary.

   (A) 10.25 cm

   (B) 15.26 cm

   (C) 25 cm

   (D) 21 cm

   (E) 14.28 cm

4. *Multiple Choice*   Find the value of x.

   (A) 5   (B) $2\sqrt{5}$

   (C) $5\sqrt{2}$ (D) 7

   (E) 7.5

5. *Multiple Choice*   Find the area of the figure.

   (A) 260 ft²   (B) 130 ft²

   (C) 240 ft²   (D) 120 ft²

   (E) 140 ft²

6. *Multiple Choice*   Find the area of the figure. Round to the nearest tenth, if necessary.

   (A) 307.5 m²

   (B) 410 m²

   (C) 585 m²

   (D) 615 m²

   (E) 1230 m²

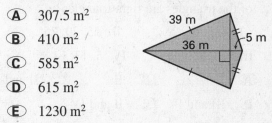

7. *Multiple Choice*   Find the area of the figure. Round to the nearest hundredth, if necessary.

   (A) 79.37 m²

   (B) 53.61 m²

   (C) 75 m²

   (D) 57.0 m²

   (E) 40.74 m²

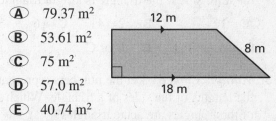

8. *Quantitative Comparison*   Use the diagram below to find the variables. Choose the statement below that is true about the given values.

   (A) The value of column A is greater.

   (B) The value of column B is greater.

   (C) The two values are equal.

   (D) The relationship cannot be determined from the given information.

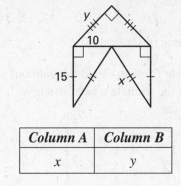

Column A	Column B
x	y

NAME _____ DATE _____

Standardized Test Practice

For use with pages 543–549

TEST TAKING STRATEGY   **Avoid spending too much time on one question. Skip questions that are too difficult for you, and spend no more than a few minutes on each question.**

1. *Multiple Choice*   Let the numbers represent the lengths of the sides of a triangle. Which of the triangles are right triangles?

   I. 4, 5, 6   II. 15, 20, 25

   III. 15, 36, 39   IV. 5, 13, 14

   (A) I   (B) II   (C) II and III

   (D) III and IV   (E) II and IV

2. *Multiple Choice*   If two sides of a triangle are 8 and 10, what measurement could represent the third side if the triangle is a right triangle?

   (A) 12   (B) $2\sqrt{41}$ (C) 6

   (D) A or B   (E) B or C

3. *Multiple Choice*   Let the numbers represent the lengths of the sides of a triangle. Which of the triangles are acute triangles?

   I. 10, 24, 26   II. 6, 8, 9.5

   III. 12, 17, 22   IV. 45, 60, 75

   (A) I and II   (B) II   (C) II and III

   (D) III   (E) III and IV

4. *Multiple Choice*   Which set of numbers can represent the side lengths of an obtuse triangle?

   (A) 2, 3, 4   (B) 3, 5, $\sqrt{34}$

   (C) 3, 7, 7.5   (D) 12, 15, $3\sqrt{41}$

   (E) none of these

5. *Multiple Choice*   Find the value of x that makes the triangle a right triangle.

   (A) 12
   (B) 13
   (C) 15
   (D) 17
   (E) 20

   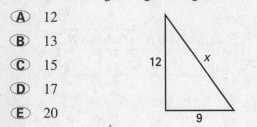

6. *Multiple Choice*   Find the value of y that makes the triangle an acute triangle.

   (A) 20   (B) 18.5

   (C) 18   (D) 17

   (E) 16

7. *Multiple Choice*   Given points $P(-2, 4)$ and $Q(2, 6)$ are two vertices in a right triangle, which point could represent the third vertex?

   (A) $(0, 9)$ (B) $(4, 2)$ (C) $(0, 0)$

   (D) B and C   (E) none of these

Quantitative Comparison   **In Exercises 8 and 9, choose the statement below that is true about the given values.**

   (A) The value in column A is greater.
   (B) The value in column B is greater.
   (C) The values are equal.
   (D) The relationship cannot be determined from the given information.

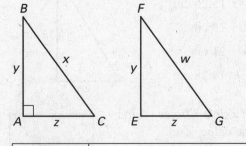

	Column A	Column B
8.	x	w when $\triangle EFG$ is acute
9.	x	w when $\triangle EFG$ is obtuse

Chapter 9

NAME _____ DATE _____

Standardized Test Practice

For use with pages 551–557

TEST TAKING STRATEGY **Staying physically relaxed during the SAT is very important. If you find yourself tensing up, put your pencil down and take a couple of deep breaths. This will help you stay calm.**

1. *Multiple Choice* Find the values of x and y.

(A) $x = 6, y = 6\sqrt{3}$

(B) $x = 3\sqrt{2}, y = 6\sqrt{2}$

(C) $x = 2\sqrt{3}, y = 4\sqrt{3}$

(D) $x = 6, y = 6\sqrt{2}$

(E) $x = 6\sqrt{2}, y = 6$

2. *Multiple Choice* Find the values of a and b.

(A) $a = 9, b = 9\sqrt{2}$

(B) $a = 18, b = 9\sqrt{3}$

(C) $a = 9\sqrt{3}, b = 18$

(D) $a = 3\sqrt{3}, b = 6\sqrt{3}$

(E) $a = 6\sqrt{3}, b = 3\sqrt{3}$

3. *Multiple Choice* Find the values of x and y.

(A) $x = 3\sqrt{2}, y = 3$

(B) $x = 3, y = 3\sqrt{2}$

(C) $x = \sqrt{2}, y = 3\sqrt{2}$

(D) $x = 3\sqrt{2}, y = \sqrt{2}$

(E) $x = \sqrt{2}, y = 3$

4. *Multiple Choice* Find the values of m and n.

(A) $m = \dfrac{16\sqrt{3}}{3}, n = \dfrac{8\sqrt{3}}{3}$

(B) $m = 16, n = 8\sqrt{3}$

(C) $m = \dfrac{8\sqrt{3}}{3}, n = \dfrac{16\sqrt{3}}{3}$

(D) $m = 16\sqrt{3}, n = 16$

(E) $m = 8\sqrt{3}, n = 16$

5. *Multiple Choice* Find the value of x.

(A) $\dfrac{5\sqrt{2}}{2}$ **(B)** $10\sqrt{2}$

(C) $5\sqrt{2}$ **(D)** 5

(E) $\dfrac{10}{\sqrt{2}}$

6. *Multiple Choice* Find the area of the figure. Round to the nearest tenth if necessary.

(A) 68.2 m^2 **(B)** 93.5 m^2

(C) 70.1 m^2 **(D)** 140.3 m^2

(E) 187.0 m^2

7. *Multiple Choice* The perimeter of a square is 54 cm. Find the length of a diagonal, rounding to the nearest tenth.

(A) 10.4 cm **(B)** 19.1 cm **(C)** 13.5 cm

(D) 22.4 cm **(E)** 38.2 cm

8. *Multiple Choice* The side of an equilateral triangle is 12 cm. Find the length of an altitude of the triangle.

(A) $6\sqrt{3}$ cm **(B)** $6\sqrt{2}$ cm **(C)** 6 cm

(D) $12\sqrt{3}$ cm **(E)** $12\sqrt{2}$ cm

9. *Multi-Step Problem* $\triangle ABC$ is equilateral and $DEGF$ is a square.

a. Find DG.

b. Find DI.

c. Find DJ.

d. Find DB.

e. Find BJ.

f. Find the area of trapezoid $ADEG$. Round to the nearest tenth.

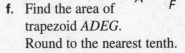

TEST TAKING STRATEGY   If you find yourself spending too much time on one test question and getting frustrated, move on to the next question. You can revisit a difficult problem later with a fresh perspective.

1. Multiple Choice   Use the triangle below. Choose the correct ratio to find tan B.

Ⓐ $\dfrac{b}{a}$ Ⓑ $\dfrac{a}{b}$

Ⓒ $\dfrac{a}{c}$ Ⓓ $\dfrac{c}{a}$

Ⓔ $\dfrac{b}{c}$

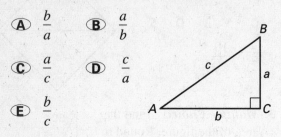

2. Multiple Choice   Find the sine of $\angle A$.

Ⓐ 0.3846   Ⓑ 0.4167

Ⓒ 0.9231   Ⓓ 1.0833

Ⓔ 2.4

3. Multiple Choice   Find the cosine of $\angle B$.

Ⓐ 1.7321

Ⓑ 0.8660

Ⓒ 2

Ⓓ 1.1547

Ⓔ 0.5774

4. Multiple Choice   Use the diagram in Exercise 3 to find the tangent of $\angle B$.

Ⓐ 1.7321   Ⓑ 0.8660   Ⓒ 2

Ⓓ 1.1547   Ⓔ 0.5774

5. Multiple Choice   Find the value of x.

Ⓐ 16 sin 35°

Ⓑ 16 cos 35°

Ⓒ $\dfrac{\sin 35°}{16}$

Ⓓ $\dfrac{16}{\sin 35°}$

Ⓔ 16 tan 35°

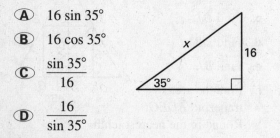

6. Multiple Choice   Find the perimeter of the triangle. Round to the nearest tenth.

Ⓐ 42.2 in.

Ⓑ 39.9 in.

Ⓒ 37.2 in.

Ⓓ 39.1 in.

Ⓔ 33.1 in.

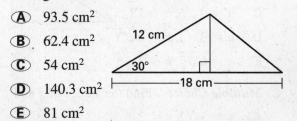

7. Multiple Choice   Find the area of the triangle. Round to the nearest tenth.

Ⓐ 93.5 cm²

Ⓑ 62.4 cm²

Ⓒ 54 cm²

Ⓓ 140.3 cm²

Ⓔ 81 cm²

Quantitative Comparison   In Exercises 8 and 9, choose the statement below that is true about the given values.

Ⓐ The value in column A is greater.

Ⓑ The value in column B is greater.

Ⓒ The two values are equal.

Ⓓ The relationship cannot be determined from the given information.

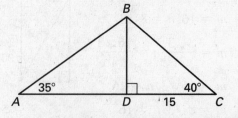

	Column A	Column B
8.	AD	BC
9.	$BD + AB$	$AD + BC$

Geometry
Standardized Test Practice Workbook

Chapter 9

NAME _____ DATE _____

Standardized Test Practice

For use with pages 567–572

TEST TAKING STRATEGY   The mathematical portion of the SAT is based on material taught in your high school mathematics courses. One of the best ways to prepare for the SAT is to keep up with your regular studies and do your homework.

1. **Multiple Choice**   Which statements below are true?

   I. You can solve a right triangle if you are given the lengths of two sides.

   II. You can solve a right triangle if you are given the measure of the two acute angles.

   III. You can solve a right triangle if you are given only one side and one acute angle.

   Ⓐ I   Ⓑ II   Ⓒ III

   Ⓓ I and III   Ⓔ all of these

2. **Multiple Choice**   Which is the approximate measure of acute $\angle A$ when $\tan A = 0.698$?

   Ⓐ 44.3°   Ⓑ 12.2°   Ⓒ 34.9°

   Ⓓ 45.7°   Ⓔ 35.2°

3. **Multiple Choice**   In the diagram below, what is the measure of $\angle M$, rounded to the nearest tenth?

   Ⓐ 63.6°
   Ⓑ 63.4°
   Ⓒ 26.6°
   Ⓓ 26.4°
   Ⓔ 63.5°

   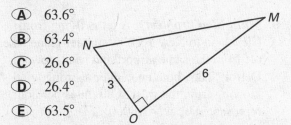

4. **Multiple Choice**   In the diagram below, find the measure of $\angle Z$. Round to the nearest tenth.

   Ⓐ 48.6°
   Ⓑ 28.1°
   Ⓒ 61.9°
   Ⓓ 41.4°
   Ⓔ 29.6°

   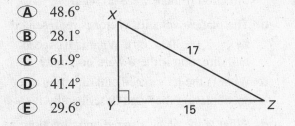

5. **Multiple Choice**   In the diagram in Exercise 4, find the measure of $\overline{XY}$.

   Ⓐ 6   Ⓑ 10   Ⓒ 7

   Ⓓ 9   Ⓔ 8

6. **Multiple Choice**   In the diagram below, what are the measures of $\overline{AB}$ and $\overline{CB}$, rounded to the nearest tenth?

   Ⓐ $AB = 46.9$, $CB = 41.4$
   Ⓑ $AB = 24.9$, $CB = 46.9$
   Ⓒ $AB = 46.9$, $CB = 24.9$
   Ⓓ $AB = 24.9$, $CB = 41.4$
   Ⓔ $AB = 41.4$, $CB = 46.9$

   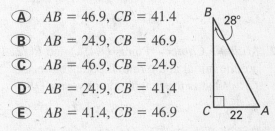

Quantitative Comparison   **In Exercises 7–9, use the diagram below to find the values. Choose the statement below which is true about the given value.**

   Ⓐ The value in column A is greater.
   Ⓑ The value in column B is greater.
   Ⓒ The two values are equal.
   Ⓓ The relationship cannot be determined from the given information.

   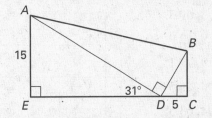

	Column A	Column B
7.	AD	AB
8.	DB	BC
9.	$ED + BC$	$AD + BC$

NAME _____ DATE _____

Standardized Test Practice

TEST TAKING STRATEGY   **Make sure that you are familiar with the directions before taking a standardized test.**

1. *Multiple Choice*   Points $M(7, -1)$ and $N(2, -8)$ are the initial and terminal points of vector $\overrightarrow{MN}$. Which choice below is the component form of $\overrightarrow{MN}$?

   Ⓐ $\langle 5, 7 \rangle$ Ⓑ 12.7   Ⓒ $\langle 9, -9 \rangle$

   Ⓓ $\langle -5, -7 \rangle$ Ⓔ $\langle 9, -7 \rangle$

2. *Multiple Choice*   Points $Q(4, 1)$ and $R(12, 4)$ are the initial and terminal points of vector $\overrightarrow{QR}$. What is the magnitude of vector $\overrightarrow{QR}$?

   Ⓐ 8.5   Ⓑ $\langle 8, 3 \rangle$ Ⓒ $\langle -8, -3 \rangle$

   Ⓓ 16.8   Ⓔ $\langle 16, 5 \rangle$

3. *Multiple Choice*   Points $A(-3, 2)$ and $B(-6, -8)$ are the initial and terminal points of vector $\overrightarrow{BA}$. What is its magnitude?

   Ⓐ $\langle 3, 10 \rangle$ Ⓑ $\langle -9, -6 \rangle$ Ⓒ 10.4

   Ⓓ 10.6   Ⓔ 10.8

4. *Multiple Choice*   Use the diagram below to find the magnitude and direction of $\overrightarrow{EF}$.

   Ⓐ 11.3, 69.3°

   Ⓑ 17.9, 12.9°

   Ⓒ 17.9, 77.1°

   Ⓓ 8.94, 26.5°

   Ⓔ 8.94, 63.5°

   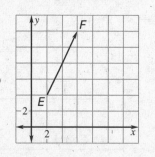

5. *Multiple Choice*   Let $\vec{J} = \langle 5, -1 \rangle$ and $\vec{K} = \langle 15, 3 \rangle$. What is $\vec{J} + \vec{K}$?

   Ⓐ $\langle 10, 4 \rangle$ Ⓑ $\langle 20, 2 \rangle$

   Ⓒ $\langle -10, -4 \rangle$ Ⓓ $\langle 10, 2 \rangle$

   Ⓔ $\langle 20, 4 \rangle$

6. *Multiple Choice*   Let $\vec{P} = \langle 7, -2 \rangle$ and $\vec{Q} = \langle -5, 8 \rangle$. What is the component form and magnitude of $\vec{P} + \vec{Q}$, rounded to the nearest tenth?

   Ⓐ $\langle 2, 6 \rangle, 6.3$ Ⓑ $\langle 2, -6 \rangle, 6.3$

   Ⓒ $\langle 12, -10 \rangle, 15.6$ Ⓓ $\langle -2, 6 \rangle, 6.3$

   Ⓔ $\langle -12, 10 \rangle, 15.6$

7. *Multiple Choice*   Let $\vec{A} = \langle x, 4 \rangle$ and $\vec{B} = \langle 14, y \rangle$. If $\vec{A} + \vec{B} = \langle 12, 6 \rangle$, what are the values of x and y?

   Ⓐ $x = -2, y = 10$ Ⓑ $x = -2, y = 2$

   Ⓒ $x = 2, y = 10$ Ⓓ $x = 2, y = -2$

   Ⓔ $x = -2, y = -10$

8. *Multiple Choice*   Vector $\overrightarrow{XY} = \langle 5, 9 \rangle$. Which vector below has the same magnitude but a different direction?

   Ⓐ $\langle -3, 2 \rangle$ Ⓑ $\langle -4, 10 \rangle$ Ⓒ $\langle 10, 18 \rangle$

   Ⓓ $\langle 4, 10 \rangle$ Ⓔ $\langle -5, 9 \rangle$

9. *Multi-Step Problem*   A jet is flying from Cleveland to New York. A smaller plane takes off from the same airport and heads towards Detroit. They both encounter a strong wind blowing from the west at 80 miles per hour, represented by $\vec{w} = \langle 80, 0 \rangle$.

   a. The jet's velocity vector is represented by $\vec{j} = \langle 450, 510 \rangle$. What is its speed and direction if there were no wind?

   b. The plane's velocity vector is represented by $\vec{p} = \langle -300, 200 \rangle$. What is its speed and direction if there were no wind?

   c. What is the jet's speed and direction after encountering the wind described by $\vec{w}$?

   d. What is the plane's speed and direction after encountering the wind described by $\vec{w}$?

Geometry
Standardized Test Practice Workbook

Standardized Test Practice

For use with pages 595–602

TEST TAKING STRATEGY   Sketch graphs or figures in your test booklet to help you solve the problems. Even though you must keep your answer sheet neat, you can make any kind of mark you want in your test booklet.

For Exercises 1–5, use the diagram below.

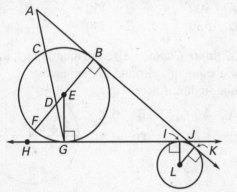

1. *Multiple Choice* $\overline{FB}$ is best described as a

   Ⓐ radius.   Ⓑ diameter.

   Ⓒ chord.   Ⓓ secant.

   Ⓔ tangent.

2. *Multiple Choice* $\overleftrightarrow{AJ}$ is best described as a

   Ⓐ diameter.   Ⓑ secant.

   Ⓒ chord.

   Ⓓ common external tangent.

   Ⓔ common internal tangent.

3. *Multiple Choice* $\overleftrightarrow{CD}$ is best described as a

   Ⓐ diameter.   Ⓑ secant.

   Ⓒ chord.

   Ⓓ common external tangent.

   Ⓔ common internal tangent.

4. *Multiple Choice* $\overline{CG}$ is best described as a

   Ⓐ diameter.   Ⓑ radius.

   Ⓒ secant.   Ⓓ tangent.

   Ⓔ chord.

5. *Multiple Choice* $\overleftrightarrow{HJ}$ is best described as a

   Ⓐ secant.   Ⓑ chord.

   Ⓒ common external tangent.   Ⓓ common internal tangent.

   Ⓔ diameter.

6. *Multiple Choice* What is the diameter of ⊙C?

   Ⓐ 8   Ⓑ 4

   Ⓒ 3   Ⓓ 2

   Ⓔ 5

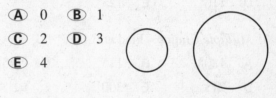

7. *Multiple Choice* How many common tangents do the circles have?

   Ⓐ 0   Ⓑ 1

   Ⓒ 2   Ⓓ 3

   Ⓔ 4

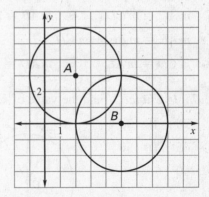

8. *Multi-Step Problem* Use the diagram below to answer parts (a)–(d).

   a. What is the center and radius of ⊙A?

   b. What is the center and radius of ⊙B?

   c. What is the intersection of the circles?

   d. Tell whether the common tangents are internal or external.

NAME _____ DATE _____

Standardized Test Practice

For use with pages 603–611

TEST TAKING STRATEGY   **Do not panic if you run out of time before answering all of the questions. You can still receive a high test score without answering every question.**

For Exercises 1–4, use the circle at the right.

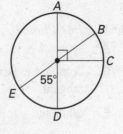

1. *Multiple Choice*   Find $m\overset{\frown}{BC}$.

  A 55°   **B** 90°   **C** 35°

  D 110°   **E** 125°

2. *Multiple Choice*   Find $m\overset{\frown}{CD}$.

  A 55°   **B** 90°   **C** 35°

  D 110°   **E** 125°

3. *Multiple Choice*   Find $m\overset{\frown}{CAE}$.

  A 180°   **B** 125°   **C** 145°

  D 215°   **E** 300°

4. *Multiple Choice*   Which statement is *not* true?

  A $m\overset{\frown}{AC} = m\overset{\frown}{CD}$ **B** $m\overset{\frown}{AB} = m\overset{\frown}{ED}$

  C $m\overset{\frown}{AE} = m\overset{\frown}{BC} + m\overset{\frown}{CD}$

  D $m\overset{\frown}{CD} = m\overset{\frown}{AE}$ **E** $m\overset{\frown}{AD} = m\overset{\frown}{EB}$

5. *Multiple Choice*   Find the value of x.

  A 20 **B** 30

  C 45 **D** 50

  E 60

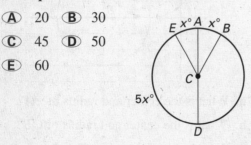

6. *Multiple Choice*   What is $m\overset{\frown}{EDB}$ in Exercise 5?

  A 100°   **B** 150°   **C** 300°

  D 330°   **E** 340°

7. *Multiple Choice*   Use the diagram to find the value of x. Round to the nearest hundredth, if necessary.

  A 4   **B** 5

  C 5.62   **D** 6.31

  E 5.83

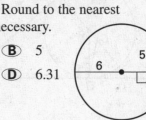

8. *Multiple Choice*   Use the diagram below to find the value of x.

  A 10 **B** 20

  C 22 **D** 11

  E 44

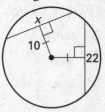

Quantitative Comparison   In Exercises 9 and 10, use the diagram to choose the statement that is true.

  A The value in column A is greater.

  B The value in column B is greater.

  C The two values are equal.

  D The relationship cannot be determined from the given information.

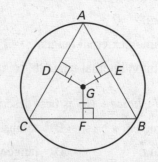

	Column A	Column B
9.	$m\angle DGE$	$m\angle DAE$
10.	$m\overset{\frown}{ABC}$	$m\overset{\frown}{CAB}$

NAME _____ DATE _____

Standardized Test Practice

For use with pages 613–620

TEST TAKING STRATEGY   **If you find yourself spending too much time on one test question and getting frustrated, move on to the next question. You can revisit a difficult problem later with a fresh perspective.**

1. *Multiple Choice*
What is $m\,\widehat{AB}$?

- Ⓐ 10° Ⓑ 20°
- Ⓒ 30° Ⓓ 40°
- Ⓔ 60°

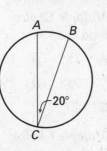

2. *Multiple Choice*   If an inscribed angle has a measure of 100°, what is the measure of the intercepted arc?

- Ⓐ 100°   Ⓑ 200°   Ⓒ 50°
- Ⓓ 0°   Ⓔ 180°

3. *Multiple Choice*   Find the value of x.

- Ⓐ 178 Ⓑ 356
- Ⓒ 89   Ⓓ 182
- Ⓔ 91

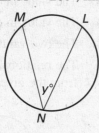

4. *Multiple Choice*   If $m\,\widehat{LNM} = 280°$, find the value of y.

- Ⓐ 40   Ⓑ 80
- Ⓒ 160 Ⓓ 140
- Ⓔ 280

5. *Multiple Choice*   Find the values of a and b.

- Ⓐ $a = 50, b = 50$
- Ⓑ $a = 25, b = 50$
- Ⓒ $a = 50, b = 25$
- Ⓓ $a = 25, b = 25$
- Ⓔ $a = 100, b = 25$

6. *Multiple Choice*   Find the value of x.

- Ⓐ 5   Ⓑ 3
- Ⓒ 8   Ⓓ 10
- Ⓔ 7.5

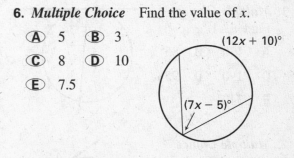

7. *Multiple Choice*   Find the values of x and y.

- Ⓐ $x = 80, y = 75$
- Ⓑ $x = 105, y = 100$
- Ⓒ $x = 75, y = 80$
- Ⓓ $x = 100, y = 105$
- Ⓔ $x = 90, y = 115$

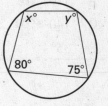

8. *Multiple Choice*   Find the values of x and y.

- Ⓐ $x = 6, y = 84$
- Ⓑ $x = 42, y = 48$
- Ⓒ $x = 42, y = 42$
- Ⓓ $x = 90, y = 84$
- Ⓔ $x = 48, y = 42$

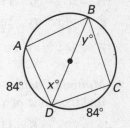

Quantitative Comparison   In Exercises 9 and 10, use the diagram to choose the statement below that is true.

- Ⓐ The value in column A is greater.
- Ⓑ The value in column B is greater.
- Ⓒ The two values are equal.
- Ⓓ The relationship cannot be determined from the given information.

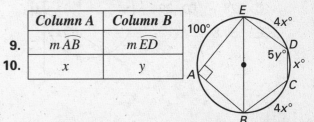

	Column A	Column B
9.	$m\,\widehat{AB}$	$m\,\widehat{ED}$
10.	x	y

LESSON

10.4

Chapter 10

NAME _____ DATE _____

Standardized Test Practice

For use with pages 621–627

TEST TAKING STRATEGY **The mathematical portion of the SAT is based on material taught in your high school mathematics courses. One of the best ways to prepare for the SAT is to keep up with your regular studies and do your homework.**

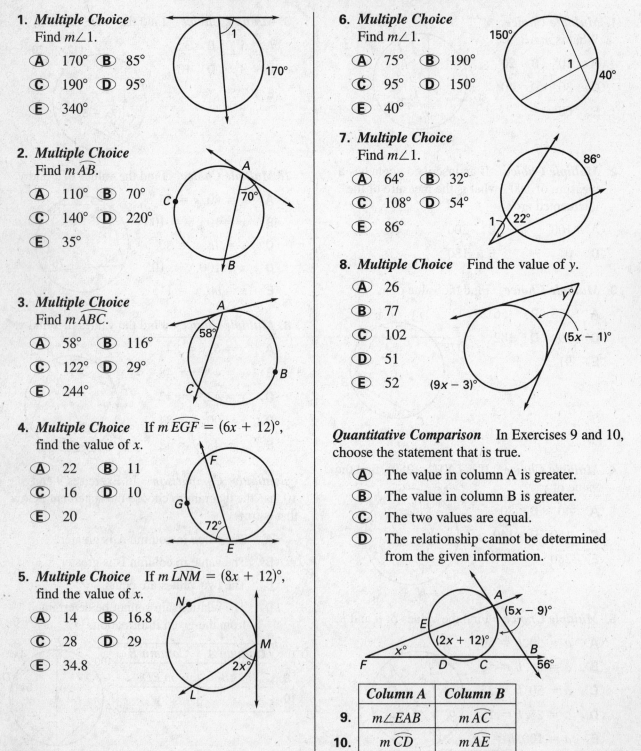

1. Multiple Choice Find $m\angle 1$.

  Ⓐ 170° Ⓑ 85°

  Ⓒ 190° Ⓓ 95°

  Ⓔ 340°

2. Multiple Choice Find $m\,\widehat{AB}$.

  Ⓐ 110° Ⓑ 70°

  Ⓒ 140° Ⓓ 220°

  Ⓔ 35°

3. Multiple Choice Find $m\,\widehat{ABC}$.

  Ⓐ 58° Ⓑ 116°

  Ⓒ 122° Ⓓ 29°

  Ⓔ 244°

4. Multiple Choice If $m\,\widehat{EGF} = (6x + 12)°$, find the value of x.

  Ⓐ 22 Ⓑ 11

  Ⓒ 16 Ⓓ 10

  Ⓔ 20

5. Multiple Choice If $m\,\widehat{LNM} = (8x + 12)°$, find the value of x.

  Ⓐ 14 Ⓑ 16.8

  Ⓒ 28 Ⓓ 29

  Ⓔ 34.8

6. Multiple Choice Find $m\angle 1$.

  Ⓐ 75° Ⓑ 190°

  Ⓒ 95° Ⓓ 150°

  Ⓔ 40°

7. Multiple Choice Find $m\angle 1$.

  Ⓐ 64° Ⓑ 32°

  Ⓒ 108° Ⓓ 54°

  Ⓔ 86°

8. Multiple Choice Find the value of y.

  Ⓐ 26

  Ⓑ 77

  Ⓒ 102

  Ⓓ 51

  Ⓔ 52

Quantitative Comparison In Exercises 9 and 10, choose the statement that is true.

  Ⓐ The value in column A is greater.

  Ⓑ The value in column B is greater.

  Ⓒ The two values are equal.

  Ⓓ The relationship cannot be determined from the given information.

	Column A	Column B
9.	$m\angle EAB$	$m\,\widehat{AC}$
10.	$m\,\widehat{CD}$	$m\,\widehat{AE}$

Geometry
Standardized Test Practice Workbook

NAME _____ DATE _____

Standardized Test Practice

For use with pages 629–635

TEST TAKING STRATEGY Make sure that you are familiar with the directions before taking a standardized test. This way, you do not need to worry about the directions during the test.

1. *Multiple Choice*
Find the value of *x*.

(A) 3   (B) 4

(C) 5   (D) 6

(E) 8

2. *Multiple Choice*
Find the value of *y*.

(A) 2   (B) 3

(C) 4   (D) 5

(E) 6

3. *Multiple Choice*
Find the value of *x*.

(A) 10   (B) 5

(C) 9.6   (D) 12

(E) 14

4. *Multiple Choice*
Find the value of *x*.

(A) 3.2   (B) 12.8

(C) 4.9   (D) 7.8

(E) 1.8

5. *Multiple Choice* Find the value of *x*. Round to the nearest tenth, if necessary.

(A) 22   (B) 8.8

(C) 5.3   (D) 6.6

(E) 14

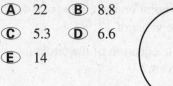

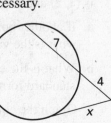

6. *Multiple Choice* You are standing 16 feet from a circular swimming pool. The distance from you to a point of tangency is 25 feet. What is the approximate diameter of the pool?

(A) 23 ft   (B) 46 ft   (C) 19 ft

(D) 38 ft   (E) 15 ft

7. *Multiple Choice* Find the values of *x* and *y*. Round to the nearest tenth, if necessary.

(A) $x = 14.4, y = 18$

(B) $x = 12, y = 8$

(C) $x = 14.4, y = 8$

(D) $x = 12, y = 18$

(E) $x = 24, y = 8$

Quantitative Comparison In Exercises 8 and 9, use the diagram to choose the statement below that is true.

(A) The value in column A is greater.

(B) The value in column B is greater.

(C) The two values are equal.

(D) The relationship cannot be determined from the given information.

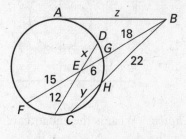

	Column A	Column B
8.	*x*	*y*
9.	*z*	*HB*

LESSON

10.6

Chapter 10

NAME _____ DATE _____

Standardized Test Practice

For use with pages 636–640

TEST TAKING STRATEGY   **Work as quickly as you can through the easier sections, but avoid making careless errors on easy questions.**

1. *Multiple Choice*   What is the standard form of the equation of a circle with center $(3, -2)$ and radius 4?

   Ⓐ $(x - 3)^2 + (y - 2)^2 = 4$
   Ⓑ $(x - 3)^2 + (y - 2)^2 = 16$
   Ⓒ $(x - 3)^2 + (y - 2)^2 = 8$
   Ⓓ $(x + 3)^2 + (y + 2)^2 = 16$
   Ⓔ $(x - 3)^2 + (y + 2)^2 = 16$

2. *Multiple Choice*   What is the center of a circle with an equation of $(x + 5)^2 + (y - 1)^2 = 36$?

   Ⓐ $(6, 0)$ Ⓑ $(0, 6)$
   Ⓒ $(-5, 1)$ Ⓓ $(-5, -1)$
   Ⓔ $(5, 1)$

3. *Multiple Choice*   What is the radius of a circle with an equation of $\left(x - \frac{4}{9}\right)^2 + \left(y - \frac{9}{16}\right)^2 = \frac{25}{36}$?

   Ⓐ $\frac{2}{3}$ Ⓑ $\frac{4}{9}$ Ⓒ $\frac{3}{4}$
   Ⓓ $\frac{5}{6}$ Ⓔ $\frac{25}{36}$

4. *Multiple Choice*   What is the center and radius of the circle in the diagram?

   Ⓐ $(1, 4), 2$
   Ⓑ $(4, 3), 2$
   Ⓒ $(3, 4), 2$
   Ⓓ $(4, 3), 4$
   Ⓔ $(3, 4), 4$

   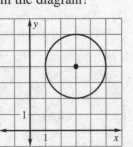

5. *Multiple Choice*   What is the equation of the circle in Exercise 4?

   Ⓐ $(x + 4)^2 + (y + 3)^2 = 2$
   Ⓑ $(x - 3)^2 + (y - 4)^2 = 2$
   Ⓒ $(x + 4)^2 + (y + 3)^2 = 4$
   Ⓓ $(x - 3)^2 + (y - 4)^2 = 4$
   Ⓔ $(x - 1)^2 + (y - 4)^2 = 4$

6. *Multiple Choice*   The center of a circle is $(2, 4)$ and a point on the circle is $(-1, 4)$. What is the equation of the circle?

   Ⓐ $(x + 4)^2 + (y + 2)^2 = 9$
   Ⓑ $(x - 2)^2 + (y - 4)^2 = 9$
   Ⓒ $(x + 2)^2 + (y + 4)^2 = 9$
   Ⓓ $(x + 2)^2 + (y + 4)^2 = 3$
   Ⓔ $(x - 2)^2 + (y - 4)^2 = 3$

7. *Multiple Choice*   A diameter of a circle has endpoints of $(-5, 6)$ and $(-5, -2)$. What is the equation of the circle?

   Ⓐ $(x + 5)^2 + (y - 2)^2 = 16$
   Ⓑ $(x - 5)^2 + (y + 2)^2 = 4$
   Ⓒ $(x + 5)^2 + (y - 2)^2 = 4$
   Ⓓ $(x + 5)^2 + (y - 2)^2 = 64$
   Ⓔ $(x + 5)^2 + (y - 4)^2 = 4$

8. *Multiple Choice*   The center of a circle is $(5, -3)$ and its radius is 4. Which point lies on the *exterior* of the circle?

   Ⓐ $(4, -2)$ Ⓑ $(6, 0)$
   Ⓒ $(4, -5)$ Ⓓ $(-1, -4)$
   Ⓔ $(1, -3)$

9. *Multi-Step Problem*   The center of a circle is $(x, 2)$ and its radius is 3. Assume $x > -4$.

   a. If another point on the circle is $(-4, 2)$, what is the value of x?

   b. What is the equation of the circle in standard form?

   c. Graph the equation from part (b).

   d. Name a point *on* the circle, a point in the *interior* of the circle, and a point in the *exterior* of the circle.

NAME _____ DATE _____

Standardized Test Practice

For use with pages 642–648

TEST TAKING STRATEGY **It is important to remember that your SAT score will not solely determine your acceptance into a college or university. Do not put added pressure on yourself to do well. If you are not satisfied with your SAT score, remember that you can take it again.**

1. *Multiple Choice* What is the locus of all points in the coordinate plane that are equidistant from points $(3, 2)$ and $(3, 16)$?

   Ⓐ The line $x = 9$ Ⓑ The line $y = 9$

   Ⓒ $(3, 9)$ Ⓓ The line $x = 3$

   Ⓔ $(3, 14)$ and $(3, 18)$

2. *Multiple Choice* What is the locus of all points in the coordinate plane that are equidistant from points $A(1, -2)$ and $B(3, -2)$ and are $\sqrt{5}$ units from B.

   Ⓐ The line $x = 2$ Ⓑ The line $y = 2$

   Ⓒ $\left(2, -3\sqrt{2}\right), \left(2, 2\sqrt{2}\right)$

   Ⓓ $\left(2, \sqrt{2}\right), \left(2, -4\sqrt{2}\right)$

   Ⓔ $(2, 0), (2, -4)$

3. *Multiple Choice* What is the locus of all points that are equidistant from the lines $y = \frac{3}{5}x + 2$ and $3x - 5y = -50$.

   Ⓐ $(0, 6)$

   Ⓑ The line $y = \frac{3}{5}x + 4$

   Ⓒ The line $y = \frac{3}{5}x + 6$

   Ⓓ $(0, 6)$ and $(-10, 0)$

   Ⓔ The lines $y = \frac{3}{5}x + 12$ and $y = \frac{3}{5}x$

4. *Multiple Choice* Point D is in the interior of $\angle ABC$. What is the number of possible locus points in the interior of $\angle ABC$ that are equidistance from $\angle ABC$ and 1 inch from point D?

   Ⓐ 0 points

   Ⓑ 1 point

   Ⓒ 2 points

   Ⓓ all points on the $\perp$ bisector of $\angle ABC$

   Ⓔ cannot be determined

For Exercises 5–7, use the graph at the right.

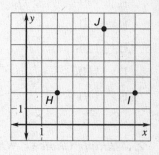

5. *Multiple Choice* Find the locus of points in the coordinate plane that are equidistant from H and I.

   Ⓐ The line $x = \frac{9}{2}$ Ⓑ The line $y = 5$

   Ⓒ The line $y = \frac{9}{2}$ Ⓓ $(5, 2)$ and $(0, 2)$

   Ⓔ $(5, 2)$

6. *Multiple Choice* Find the locus of points that are 4 units from J.

   Ⓐ $(5, 2)$ and $(5, 10)$

   Ⓑ The circle $(x + 5)^2 + (y + 6)^2 = 16$

   Ⓒ $(1, 6)$ and $(9, 6)$

   Ⓓ The circle $(x - 5)^2 + (y - 6)^2 = 8$

   Ⓔ The circle $(x - 5)^2 + (y - 6)^2 = 16$

7. *Multiple Choice* Find the locus of points that are 2 units from $\overleftrightarrow{HI}$.

   Ⓐ The line $y = 4$ Ⓑ The line $x = 4$

   Ⓒ The line $y = 0$ Ⓓ A and C

   Ⓔ A and B

8. *Multi-Step Problem* You are given seismograph readings from three locations.

   • At $A(4, 6)$, the epicenter is 10 miles away.

   • At $B(-2, -4)$, the epicenter is 6 miles away.

   • At $C(10, -4)$, the epicenter is 6 miles away.

   a. Graph points A, B, and C on a coordinate plane.

   b. What is the locus of points equidistant from A? from B? from C?

   c. Find the epicenter.

NAME _____ DATE _____

Standardized Test Practice

For use with pages 661–668

TEST TAKING STRATEGY **Staying physically relaxed during the SAT is very important. If you find yourself tensing up, put your pencil down and take a couple of deep breaths. This will help you stay calm.**

1. Multiple Choice What is the value of x?

Ⓐ 100
Ⓑ 140
Ⓒ 120
Ⓓ 150
Ⓔ 110

(figure: polygon with angles 85°, $x°$, 120°, 95°, 100°)

2. Multiple Choice What is the value of y?

Ⓐ 50
Ⓑ 100
Ⓒ 130
Ⓓ 75
Ⓔ 40

(figure: polygon with angles 130°, 75°, 125°, 145°, 115°, $y°$)

3. Multiple Choice The measure of each interior angle of a regular polygon is 144°. How many sides does the polygon have?

Ⓐ 8   Ⓑ 9   Ⓒ 10
Ⓓ 12   Ⓔ 14

4. Multiple Choice Find the value of x.

Ⓐ 31.25
Ⓑ 16.25
Ⓒ 26.25
Ⓓ 28.75
Ⓔ 13.75

(figure with angles $2x°$, $(2x + 20)°$, $3x°$, $(x + 10)°$, $(4x - 15)°$)

5. Multiple Choice A convex heptagon has interior angles that measure 120°, 115°, 135°, 95°, 155°, and 125°. What is the measure of the seventh interior angle?

Ⓐ 120°   Ⓑ 115°   Ⓒ 135°
Ⓓ 155°   Ⓔ 95°

6. Multiple Choice What is the sum of the measures of the interior angles of a convex 16-gon?

Ⓐ 1800°   Ⓑ 2340°   Ⓒ 2520°
Ⓓ 2700°   Ⓔ 2880°

7. Multiple Choice What is the measure of an exterior angle if the regular polygon has 18 sides?

Ⓐ 18°   Ⓑ 20°   Ⓒ 22°
Ⓓ 24°   Ⓔ 26°

8. Multiple Choice A convex octagon has exterior angles that measure 35°, 41°, 25°, 55°, 62°, 17°, and 38°. What is the measure of the exterior angle of the eighth vertex?

Ⓐ 267°   Ⓑ 45°   Ⓒ 177°
Ⓓ 187°   Ⓔ 87°

Quantitative Comparison In Exercises 9 and 10, choose the statement that is true.

Ⓐ The value in column A is greater.

Ⓑ The value in column B is greater.

Ⓒ The two values are equal.

Ⓓ The relationship cannot be determined from the given information.

	Column A	Column B
9.	The sum of the exterior angles of a 19-gon	The sum of the interior angles of a pentagon
10.	The number of sides of a regular polygon with an exterior angle measuring 20°	The number of sides of a regular polygon whose sum of the interior angles measures 3240°

LESSON
11.2

NAME _____ DATE _____

Standardized Test Practice
For use with pages 669–675

Chapter 11

TEST TAKING STRATEGY   Avoid spending too much time on one question. Skip questions that are too difficult for you, and spend no more than
a few minutes on each question.

1. *Multiple Choice*   Find the area of the
   triangle. Round to the nearest hundredth, if
   necessary.

   Ⓐ   12 square units

   Ⓑ   31.18 square units

   Ⓒ   5.20 square units

   Ⓓ   10.41 square units

   Ⓔ   15.59 square units

   6

2. *Multiple Choice*   Find the area of the
   inscribed regular pentagon below. Round to
   the nearest tenth.

   Ⓐ   422.3 square units

   Ⓑ   341.8 square units

   Ⓒ   211.1 square units

   Ⓓ   688.7 square units

   Ⓔ   452.2 square units

   9.7

3. *Multiple Choice*   Find the measure of the
   central angles of a regular polygon with 18
   sides.

   Ⓐ   10°   Ⓑ   20°   Ⓒ   25°

   Ⓓ   30°   Ⓔ   40°

4. *Multiple Choice*   Find the perimeter of the
   regular hexagon. Round to the nearest tenth, if
   necessary.

   Ⓐ   96 units

   Ⓑ   83.1 units

   Ⓒ   166.3 units

   Ⓓ   48 units

   Ⓔ   100.5 units

   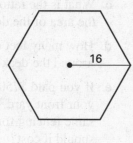

   16

5. *Multiple Choice*   Find the area and perimeter of a square with a diagonal of 10 inches.

   Ⓐ $A = 25.0$ in.^{2}, $P = 14.1$ in.

   Ⓑ $A = 28.3$ in.^{2}, $P = 50$ in.

   Ⓒ $A = 50$ in.^{2}, $P = 28.3$ in.

   Ⓓ $A = 56.6$ in.^{2}, $P = 100$ in.

   Ⓔ $A = 100$ in.^{2}, $P = 56.6$ in.

6. *Multiple Choice*   Find the area of the shaded region. The octagon is regular. Round to
   the nearest tenth, if necessary.

   Ⓐ   51.1 cm^2

   Ⓑ   408.5 cm^2

   Ⓒ   203.6 cm^2

   Ⓓ   289.0 cm^2

   Ⓔ   578.0 cm^2

   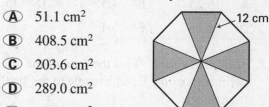

   12 cm

Quantitative Comparison   In Exercises 7
and 8, use the diagrams below to choose
the statement that is true.

   Ⓐ   The value in column A is greater.

   Ⓑ   The value in column B is greater.

   Ⓒ   The two values are equal.

   Ⓓ   The relationship cannot be determined
       from the given information.

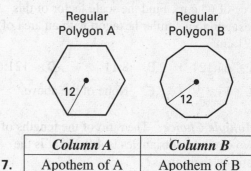

Regular
Polygon A

Regular
Polygon B

12

12

	Column A	*Column B*
7.	Apothem of A	Apothem of B
8.	Area of A	Area of B

TEST TAKING STRATEGY **When checking your work, try to use a method other than the one you originally used to get your answer. If you use the same method, you may make the same mistake twice.**

1. *Multiple Choice* A heptagon has one side length of 15 inches. Another similar heptagon has a corresponding side length of 12 inches. Find the ratio of the perimeters of the smaller to the larger heptagon.

  (A) 16:25   (B) 4:5   (C) 15:12

  (D) 25:16   (E) 5:4

2. *Multiple Choice* What is the ratio of the area of the larger heptagon to the area of the smaller heptagon in Exercise 1?

  (A) 16:25   (B) 4:5   (C) 15:12

  (D) 25:16   (E) 5:4

3. *Multiple Choice* Find the ratio of the perimeters of the larger triangle to the smaller triangle.

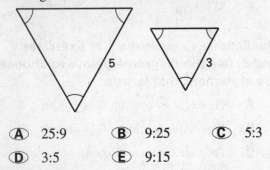

  (A) 25:9   (B) 9:25   (C) 5:3

  (D) 3:5   (E) 9:15

4. *Multiple Choice* A regular hexagon has an area of 64 cm². Find the scale factor of this hexagon to a similar hexagon with an area of 121 cm².

  (A) 64:121   (B) 8:11   (C) 121:64

  (D) 11:8   (E) None of the above

5. *Multiple Choice* The ratio of the lengths of two equilateral triangles is 4:9. What is the ratio of their areas?

  (A) 4:9   (B) 9:4   (C) 2:3

  (D) 16:81   (E) 81:16

6. *Multiple Choice* A large gazebo is shaped like a regular octagon. It has sides of length 12 feet and an area of about 696 ft². Find the area of a similar gazebo that has a perimeter of 64 feet. Round to the nearest tenth, if necessary.

  (A) 309.3 ft²   (B) 130.5 ft²

  (C) 261 ft²   (D) 116 ft²

  (E) 1566 ft²

7. *Multiple Choice* A regular pentagon has a perimeter of 25 m and an area of 43.75 m². Find the perimeter of a similar pentagon with an area of 175 m².

  (A) 100 m   (B) 75 m   (C) 25 m

  (D) 45 m   (E) 50 m

8. *Multi-Step Problem* Use the diagram of the rectangular swimming pool and deck area to answer parts (a)–(e). The rectangles are similar.

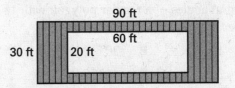

  a. What is the area of the pool?

  b. What is the area of the deck?

  c. What is the ratio of the area of the pool to the area of the deck?

  d. How many feet of fencing is needed to go around the deck?

  e. If you paid $750 for 125 feet of fencing in your front yard, and you are using the same fencing for the pool area, how much should it cost?

NAME _____ DATE _____

Standardized Test Practice

For use with pages 683–689

TEST TAKING STRATEGY   **Always look for shortcuts that will allow you to work through a problem more quickly.**

1. Multiple Choice   Find the circumference of a circle with a diameter of 16 in. Round to the nearest hundredth.

(A) 25.13 in.   (B) 50.27 in.

(C) 50.26 in.   (D) 25.14 in.

(E) 201.06 in.

2. Multiple Choice   Find the radius of a circle with a circumference of 60 m. Round to the nearest hundredth.

(A) 9.55 m   (B) 4.37 m

(C) 19.10 m   (D) 19.09 m

(E) 9.54 m

3. Multiple Choice   Find the circumference of the circle. Round to the nearest hundredth.

(A) 9.43 cm

(B) 9.42 cm

(C) 28.26 cm

(D) 18.85 cm

(E) 28.27 cm

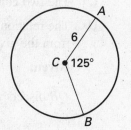

3 cm

4. Multiple Choice   Find the length of $\overparen{AB}$. Round to the nearest tenth.

(A) 6.5

(B) 14.2

(C) 13.1

(D) 8.3

(E) 6.6

A
6
C • 125°
B

5. Multiple Choice   Find the radius of ⊙ C. Round to the nearest tenth.

(A) 24.7

(B) 49.4

(C) 12.3

(D) 53.1

(E) 26.5

32.3
75°
C

6. Multiple Choice   Find the circumference of ⊙ A.

(A) 103.68

(B) 25.92

(C) 48.9

(D) 50.4

(E) 51.84

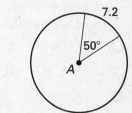

7.2
50°
A

7. Multiple Choice   Find the values of x and y.

(A) $x = 21, y \approx 4.8$

(B) $x = 25, y \approx 1.4$

(C) $x = 25, y \approx 4.8$

(D) $x = 31, y \approx 4.8$

(E) $x = 31, y \approx 1.4$

A $(3y - 5)\pi$
12
220°
C
$(5x - 15)°$ B

8. Multiple Choice   Find the perimeter of the region bounded by the circular arcs and line segments. Round to the nearest hundredth, if necessary.

(A) 114.85

(B) 77.15

(C) 102.8

(D) 46.85

(E) 66.85

3
⊢2⊣
12
3
8

9. Quantitative Comparison   **Consider the circumference of the two circles described below. Choose the statement that is true.**

(A) The quantity in column A is greater.

(B) The quantity in column B is greater.

(C) The two quantities are equal.

(D) The relationship cannot be determined from the given information.

Column A	Column B
Circle with radius 4	Circle with diameter 4

TEST TAKING STRATEGY   **Do not panic if you run out of time before answering all of the questions. You can still receive a high test score without answering every question.**

1. *Multiple Choice*   Find the area of a circle with a diameter of 7 inches. Round to the nearest hundredth.

Ⓐ 153.94 in.² Ⓑ 11.0 in.²

Ⓒ 43.98 in.² Ⓓ 19.24 in.²

Ⓔ 38.48 in.²

2. *Multiple Choice*   Find the radius of a circle with an area of 66.5 cm². Round to the nearest tenth.

Ⓐ 9.2 cm Ⓑ 5.3 cm

Ⓒ 2.3 cm Ⓓ 4.6 cm

Ⓔ 10.6 cm

3. *Multiple Choice*   Find the circumference of a circle whose area is 100 m². Round to the nearest tenth.

Ⓐ 45.4 m Ⓑ 35.4 m

Ⓒ 15.9 m Ⓓ 17.7 m

Ⓔ 31.8 m

4. *Multiple Choice*   Find the area of the sector shown in the diagram. Round to the nearest tenth.

Ⓐ 34.5 ft²

Ⓑ 36.1 ft²

Ⓒ 12.0 ft²

Ⓓ 18.1 ft²

Ⓔ 28.6 ft²

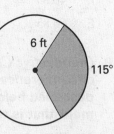

5. *Multiple Choice*   A birthday cake is cut into 16 equal pieces. If the cake has a diameter of 14 inches, what is the area of one piece of cake? Round to the nearest hundredth.

Ⓐ 38.48 in.² Ⓑ 19.2 in.²

Ⓒ 5.5 in.² Ⓓ 14.36 in.²

Ⓔ 9.62 in.²

6. *Multiple Choice*   Find the radius of ⊙ *C*, if the area of the shaded region is 47.5 cm².

Ⓐ 7 cm

Ⓑ 7.5 cm

Ⓒ 8 cm

Ⓓ 8.5 cm

Ⓔ 9 cm

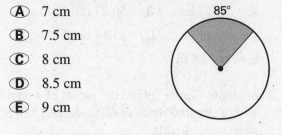

7. *Multiple Choice*   Find the area of the shaded region. The three triangles are regular. Round to the nearest tenth.

Ⓐ 67.7 cm²

Ⓑ 35.2 cm²

Ⓒ 39.3 cm²

Ⓓ 46.1 cm²

Ⓔ 56.9 cm²

Quantitative Comparison   **In Exercises 8 and 9, use the diagram below to choose the statement that is true.**

Ⓐ The value in column A is greater.

Ⓑ The value in column B is greater.

Ⓒ The two columns are equal.

Ⓓ The relationship cannot be determined from the given information.

Given:

$\overrightarrow{QB}$ bisects ∠*AQC*.

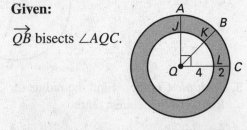

	Column A	Column B
8.	The area outlined by *ABKJ*	The area outlined by *JQL*
9.	The area of the circle with radius *JQ*.	The area of the shaded region

NAME _____ DATE _____

Standardized Test Practice

For use with pages 699–705

TEST TAKING STRATEGY   Sketch graphs of figures in your test booklet to help you solve the problems.

In Exercises 1 and 2, use the diagram below.

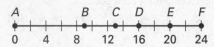

A   B   C   D   E   F
0   4   8   12   16   20   24

1. *Multiple Choice*   Find the probability that a point chosen at random on $\overline{AE}$ is on $\overline{BD}$.

   A 20%   **B** 25%   **C** 30%

   D 35%   **E** 40%

2. *Multiple Choice*   Find the probability that a point chosen at random on $\overline{BE}$ is on $\overline{CD}$. Round to the nearest hundredth.

   A 0.15   **B** 0.18   **C** 0.25

   D 0.27   **E** 0.45

3. *Multiple Choice*   Find the probability that a point chosen at random in the regular triangle lands in the shaded region.

   A 25%

   B 30%

   C $33\frac{1}{3}$%

   D 40%

   E 50%

4. *Multiple Choice*   Find the probability that a point chosen at random lands in the shaded region. Round to the nearest tenth, if necessary.

   A 39.3%

   B 60.7%

   C 64%

   D 36%

   E 37.6%

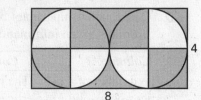

5. *Multiple Choice*   Find the probability that a point chosen at random in the circle lands in the shaded region. Round to the nearest tenth.

   A 6.9%

   B 26.8%

   C 50.0%

   D 55.6%

   E 27.8%

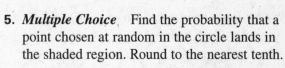

6. *Multiple Choice*   Find the probability that a point chosen at random in the hexagon lands in the shaded region. Round to the nearest hundredth.

   A 5.35%

   B 21.36%

   C 10.68%

   D 38.28%

   E 69.14%

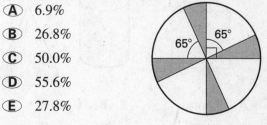

7. *Quantitative Comparison*   **Use the diagram of the game board below. A point randomly chosen in the circle is worth the number outside the sector. A point landing in the inner circle is worth double the outside value. Choose the statement below that is true about the given number.**

   A   The value in column A is greater.

   B   The value in column B is greater.

   C   The two values are equal.

   D   The relationship cannot be determined from the given information.

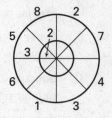

Column A	Column B
Probability of getting 4 points	Probability of getting 3 points

Chapter 11

TEST TAKING STRATEGY   **Work as quickly as you can through the easier sections, but avoid making careless errors on easy questions.**

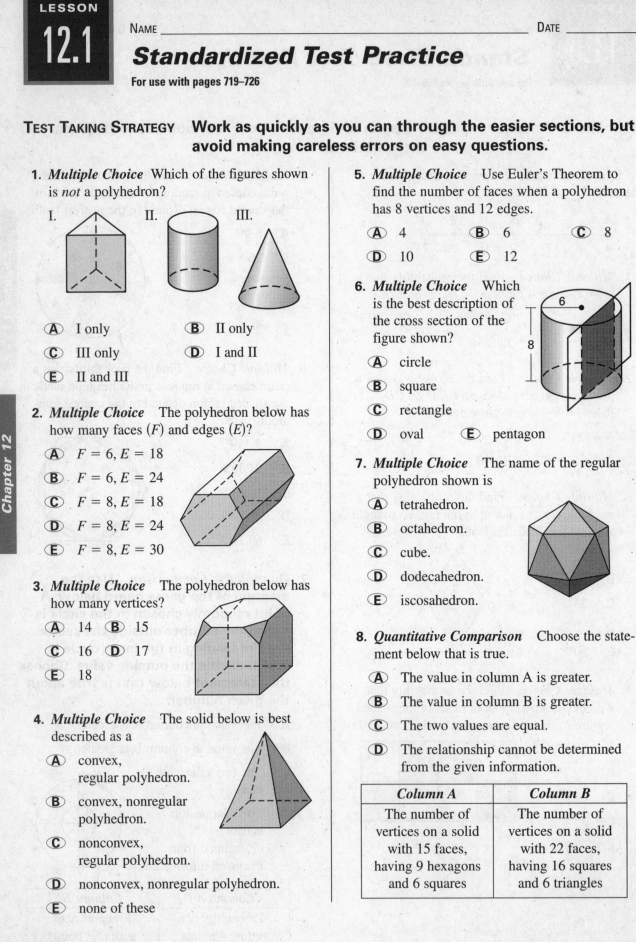

1. *Multiple Choice* Which of the figures shown is *not* a polyhedron?

   I.   II.   III.

   A I only   **B** II only

   C III only   **D** I and II

   E II and III

2. *Multiple Choice*   The polyhedron below has how many faces (*F*) and edges (*E*)?

   A $F = 6, E = 18$

   B $F = 6, E = 24$

   C $F = 8, E = 18$

   D $F = 8, E = 24$

   E $F = 8, E = 30$

3. *Multiple Choice*   The polyhedron below has how many vertices?

   A 14   **B** 15

   C 16   **D** 17

   E 18

4. *Multiple Choice*   The solid below is best described as a

   A convex, regular polyhedron.

   B convex, nonregular polyhedron.

   C nonconvex, regular polyhedron.

   D nonconvex, nonregular polyhedron.

   E none of these

5. *Multiple Choice*   Use Euler's Theorem to find the number of faces when a polyhedron has 8 vertices and 12 edges.

   A 4   **B** 6   **C** 8

   D 10   **E** 12

6. *Multiple Choice*   Which is the best description of the cross section of the figure shown?

   A circle

   B square

   C rectangle

   D oval   **E** pentagon

7. *Multiple Choice*   The name of the regular polyhedron shown is

   A tetrahedron.

   B octahedron.

   C cube.

   D dodecahedron.

   E iscosahedron.

8. *Quantitative Comparison*   Choose the statement below that is true.

   A The value in column A is greater.

   B The value in column B is greater.

   C The two values are equal.

   D The relationship cannot be determined from the given information.

Column A	Column B
The number of vertices on a solid with 15 faces, having 9 hexagons and 6 squares	The number of vertices on a solid with 22 faces, having 16 squares and 6 triangles

TEST TAKING STRATEGY **Make sure that you are familiar with the directions before taking a standardized test. This way, you do not need to worry about the directions during the test.**

1. *Multiple Choice* The best mathematical name of the solid is

(A) right prism.

(B) right rectangular prism.

(C) cube.

(D) right pentagonal prism.

(E) right hexagonal prism.

2. *Multiple Choice* How many lateral edges does the figure in Exercise 1 have?

(A) 4   (B) 5   (C) 7

(D) 15   (E) 10

3. *Multiple Choice* Find the lateral area of the right prism shown.

(A) 105 m²

(B) 90 m²

(C) 85 m²

(D) 74 m²

(E) 114 m²

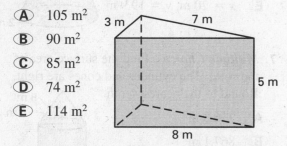

4. *Multiple Choice* Find the surface area of the regular right prism.

(A) 215 in.²

(B) 160 in.²

(C) 105 in.²

(D) 187.5 in.²

(E) 270 in.²

5. *Multiple Choice* Find the surface area of a right rectangular prism with a height of 6 inches, a length of 2 inches, and a width of 8 inches.

(A) 96 in.²   (B) 120 in.²

(C) 152 in.²   (D) 128 in.²   (E) 56 in.²

6. *Multiple Choice* Find the surface area of the right cylinder. Round to the nearest hundredth.

(A) 831.27 in.²

(B) 252 in.²

(C) 395.84 in.²

(D) 506.68 in.²

(E) 451.26 in.²

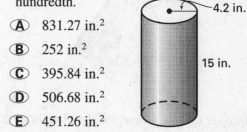

7. *Multiple Choice* Use the diagram to solve for the value of *x* given that the surface area of the figure is 286 in.².

(A) 14 in.

(B) 12 in.

(C) 6 in.

(D) 8 in.

(E) 7 in.

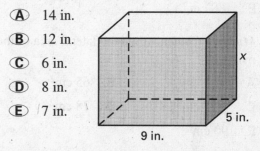

Quantitative Comparison In Exercises 8 and 9, use the solids to choose the statement below that is true.

(A) The value in column A is greater.

(B) The value in column B is greater.

(C) The two values are equal.

(D) The relationship cannot be determined from the given information.

Column A	Column B
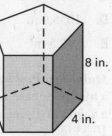	
8. Lateral area	Lateral area
9. Surface area	Surface area

NAME _____ DATE _____

Standardized Test Practice

For use with pages 735–742

TEST TAKING STRATEGY   **If you are not satisfied with your SAT score, remember that you can take it again.**

For Exercises 1–3, use the diagram below.

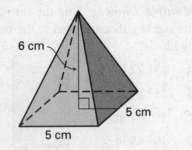

6 cm

5 cm

5 cm

1. *Multiple Choice*   Find the slant height of the pyramid.
   - Ⓐ 4.5 cm
   - Ⓑ 5.5 cm
   - Ⓒ 6.5 cm
   - Ⓓ 6 cm
   - Ⓔ 7.8 cm

2. *Multiple Choice*   Find the lateral area of the pyramid.
   - Ⓐ 57.5 cm^2
   - Ⓑ 65 cm^2
   - Ⓒ 32.5 cm^2
   - Ⓓ 78 cm^2
   - Ⓔ 90 cm^2

3. *Multiple Choice*   Find the surface area of the pyramid.
   - Ⓐ 57.5 cm^2
   - Ⓑ 65 cm^2
   - Ⓒ 32.5 cm^2
   - Ⓓ 78 cm^2
   - Ⓔ 90 cm^2

4. *Multiple Choice*   Find the slant height of the cone. Round to the nearest tenth.
   - Ⓐ 20.0   Ⓑ 10.6
   - Ⓒ 8.9   Ⓓ 14.4
   - Ⓔ 7.1

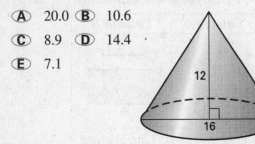

12

16

5. *Multiple Choice*   Find the surface area of the cone. Round to the nearest tenth.
   - Ⓐ 317.0 m^2
   - Ⓑ 241.7 m^2
   - Ⓒ 239.4 m^2
   - Ⓓ 278.2 m^2
   - Ⓔ 452.4 m^2

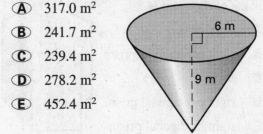

6 m

9 m

6. *Multiple Choice*   Use the diagram to solve for x and y when the surface area is 138.23 m^2.
   - Ⓐ $x = 9.8$ m, $y = 10$ m
   - Ⓑ $x = 11$ m, $y = 10.8$ m
   - Ⓒ $x = 8$ m, $y = 7.7$ m
   - Ⓓ $x = 10.8$ m, $y = 10.6$ m
   - Ⓔ $x = 20$ m, $y = 19.9$ m

y x

2 m

7. *Multiple Choice*   Find the surface area of the solid. The cylinder and cones are right. Round to the nearest tenth.
   - Ⓐ 716.3 m^2
   - Ⓑ 867.1 m^2
   - Ⓒ 1168.7 m^2
   - Ⓓ 1055.6 m^2
   - Ⓔ 942.5 m^2

8 m
6 m
15 m
6 m
8 m

8. *Multi-Step Problem*   A regular pyramid has a triangular base with a base edge of 6 inches, a height of 10 inches, and a slant height of 10.33 inches.

   a. Sketch the solid.

   b. Find the lateral area.

   c. Find the surface area.

   d. Double the lengths of the base edge, height, and slant height. What is the ratio of the surface area of the smaller pyramid to the larger pyramid?

TEST TAKING STRATEGY   **If you find yourself spending too much time on one test question and getting frustrated, move on to the next question. You can revisit a difficult problem later with a fresh perspective.**

1. *Multiple Choice*   What is the volume of a prism with a rectangular base, with sides of 5 feet and 6 feet, and a height of 4 feet?

   A 60 ft³   **B** 240 ft³

   C 120 ft³   **D** 180 ft³

   E 480 ft³

2. *Multiple Choice*   Find the value of x if the right prism has a volume of 24 m³.

   A 1 m **B** 2 m

   C 3 m **D** 4 m

   E 5 m

   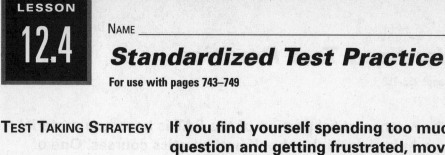

   6 m, 2 m, x

3. *Multiple Choice*   Find the volume of the right cylinder. Round the answer to the nearest hundredth.

   A 324.59 ft³

   B 216.97 ft³

   C 1996.22 ft³

   D 681.64 ft³

   E 2726.55 ft³

   4.2 ft, 12.3 ft

4. *Multiple Choice*   Find the volume of a prism that has a height of 10.5 m and has a right triangle for a base. The legs of the triangle are 5 m and 7 m. Round answer to nearest hundredth.

   A 183.75 m³   **B** 225.80 m³

   C 367.5 m³   **D** 316.14 m³

   E 180.04 m³

5. *Multiple Choice*   A cylinder has a radius of 24.6 in. and a volume of 29,468 in.³. Find its height.

   A 14.5 in.   **B** 15.5 in.   **C** 15 in.

   D 16 in.   **E** 16.5 in.

6. *Multiple Choice*   Find the volume of the oblique prism.

   A 156 cm³

   B 144 cm³   8 cm

   C 180 cm³

   D 62.4 cm³

   E 124.7 cm³

   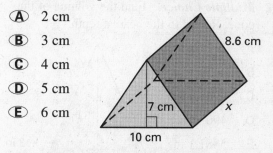

   10 cm, 6 cm, 6 cm

7. *Multiple Choice*   Find the value of x if the volume of the prism is 105 cm³.

   A 2 cm

   B 3 cm

   C 4 cm

   D 5 cm

   E 6 cm

   8.6 cm, 7 cm, x, 10 cm

8. *Multiple Choice*   Find the value of x, if the volume of the cylinder is 301.6 in.³.

   A 1.5 in.

   B 3 in.

   C 4.5 in.

   D 5 in.

   E 6 in.

   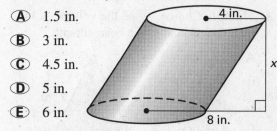

   4 in., x, 8 in.

9. *Multi-Step Problem*   You have two containers. One is a cylinder with a height of 15 inches and a diameter of 10 inches. The other side is a cube with sides of 12 inches.

   a. Sketch the containers.

   b. Find the volume of the cylinder.

   c. Find the volume of the cube.

   d. How many gallons of water are needed to fill the cylinder? (*Hint:* 1 gallon of water is 0.1337 ft³.)

Chapter 12

Standardized Test Practice

For use with pages 752–758

TEST TAKING STRATEGY **The mathematical portion of the SAT is based on material taught in your high school mathematics courses. One of the best ways to prepare for the SAT is to keep up with your regular studies and do your homework.**

1. *Multiple Choice* Find the area of the base of the pyramid. The base is a regular hexagon. Round to the nearest tenth.

- (A) 187.1 in.^{2}
- (B) 432.0 in.^{2}
- (C) 374.1 in.^{2}
- (D) 249.4 in.^{2}
- (E) 498.8 in.^{2}

18 in. 15 in. 12 in.

2. *Multiple Choice* Find the volume of the cone. Round to the nearest tenth.

- (A) 1470.3 in.^{3}
- (B) 545.3 in.^{3}
- (C) 1960.4 in.^{3}
- (D) 490.1 in.^{3}
- (E) 5881.1 in.^{3}

13 in. 12 in.

3. *Multiple Choice* Find the volume of the pyramid. Round to the nearest tenth.

- (A) 33.3 cm^3
- (B) 141.4 cm^3
- (C) 100 cm^3
- (D) 47.1 cm^3
- (E) 37.5 cm^3

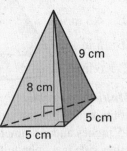

9 cm, 8 cm, 5 cm, 5 cm

4. *Multiple Choice* Find the value of x if the volume is 113.1 m^3. Round to the nearest tenth.

- (A) 1.7 m
- (B) 3.0 m
- (C) 3.1 m
- (D) 1.8 m
- (E) 2.4 m

12 cm, x

Quantitative Comparison In Exercises 5 and 6, use the diagram of the solids to choose the statement below that is true about the given values.

- (A) The value in column A is greater.
- (B) The value in column B is greater.
- (C) The two values are equal.
- (D) The relationship cannot be determined from the given information.

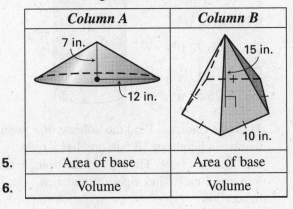

	Column A	Column B
5.	Area of base	Area of base
6.	Volume	Volume

7 in., 12 in. / 15 in., 10 in.

NAME _____ DATE _____

Standardized Test Practice

TEST TAKING STRATEGY **Staying physically relaxed during the SAT is very important. If you find yourself tensing up, put your pencil down and take a couple of deep breaths. This will help you stay calm.**

1. *Multiple Choice* If a plane contains the center of a sphere, then the intersection is called a

   Ⓐ hemisphere.   Ⓑ diameter.

   Ⓒ semi-circle.   Ⓓ great circle.

   Ⓔ half-circle.

2. *Multiple Choice* Find the surface area of the sphere. Round to the nearest tenth.

   Ⓐ 175.9 in.^{2}

   Ⓑ 615.8 in.^{2}

   Ⓒ 307.8 in.^{2}

   Ⓓ 461.8 in.^{2}

   Ⓔ 1436.8 in.^{2}

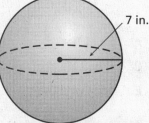

7 in.

3. *Multiple Choice* Find the volume of the sphere. Round to the nearest tenth.

   Ⓐ 44,602.2 m^3

   Ⓑ 1520.5 m^3

   Ⓒ 1393.8 m^3

   Ⓓ 5575.3 m^3

   Ⓔ 1858.4 m^3

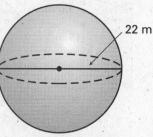

22 m

4. *Multiple Choice* What is the radius of a sphere with surface area of 1963.5 cm^2?

   Ⓐ 11 cm   Ⓑ 12.5 cm

   Ⓒ 11.5 cm   Ⓓ 12 cm

   Ⓔ 13 cm

5. *Multiple Choice* Find the circumference of the great circle if the volume of the sphere is 179.6 m^3. Round to the nearest tenth.

   Ⓐ 22 m   Ⓑ 23.8 m

   Ⓒ 11 m   Ⓓ 11.9 m

   Ⓔ 26.6 m

6. *Multiple Choice* Find the surface area of the hemisphere. Round to the nearest tenth.

   Ⓐ 706.9 cm^2

   Ⓑ 1413.7 cm^2

   Ⓒ 2120.6 cm^2

   Ⓓ 3534.3 cm^2

   Ⓔ 7775.5 cm^2

15 cm

Quantitative Comparison In Exercises 7 and 8, use the diagrams to choose the statement that is true about the given values.

   Ⓐ The value in column A is greater.

   Ⓑ The value in column B is greater.

   Ⓒ The two values are equal.

   Ⓓ The relationship cannot be determined from the given information.

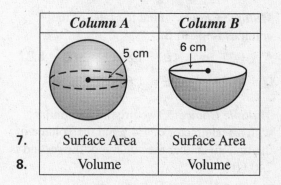

	Column A	Column B
7.	Surface Area	Surface Area
8.	Volume	Volume

Standardized Test Practice

For use with pages 766–772

TEST TAKING STRATEGY When checking your work, try to use a method other than the one you originally used to get your answer. If you use the same method, you may make the same mistake twice.

In Exercises 1–3, use the similar figures below.

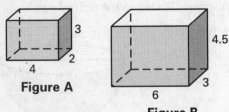

Figure A

Figure B

1. *Multiple Choice* Find the scale factor for solid A to solid B.

Ⓐ 1:2 Ⓑ 1:3 Ⓒ 1:4
Ⓓ 2:3 Ⓔ 2:5

2. *Multiple Choice* Find the ratio of the surface areas for A to B.

Ⓐ 4:9 Ⓑ 1:9 Ⓒ 4:25
Ⓓ 1:4 Ⓔ 1:16

3. *Multiple Choice* Find the ratio of the volumes for A to B.

Ⓐ 1:27 Ⓑ 1:8 Ⓒ 8:27
Ⓓ 8:125 Ⓔ 1:64

4. *Multiple Choice* Two prisms are similar with a scale factor of 1:4. Find the volume of the first given that the volume of the second is 2400 ft³.

Ⓐ 600 ft³ Ⓑ 37.5 ft³
Ⓒ 150 ft³ Ⓓ 75 ft³
Ⓔ 300 ft³

5. *Multiple Choice* Two pyramids are similar with a ratio of surface areas of 25:64. Find the volume of the second pyramid given that the first has a volume of 250 m³.

Ⓐ 61.0 m³ Ⓑ 640 m³
Ⓒ 1024 m³ Ⓓ 97.7 m³
Ⓔ 4194 m³

6. *Multiple Choice* Which solids below are similar?

I. II. III.

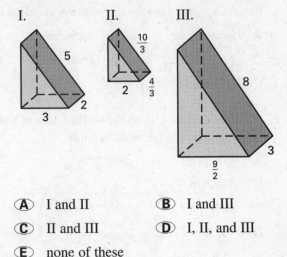

Ⓐ I and II Ⓑ I and III
Ⓒ II and III Ⓓ I, II, and III
Ⓔ none of these

7. *Multi-Step Problem* Use the similar solids shown below.

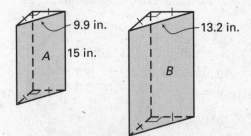

a. What is the scale factor of prism A to prism B?

b. What is the height of prism B?

c. What is the volume of prism B if the volume of prism A is 367.5 in.³?

d. What is the surface area of a third prism that is similar to A and B, and has a volume of 45.94 in.³?

NAME _____ DATE _____

Cumulative Standardized Test Practice

For use after Chapters 1–12

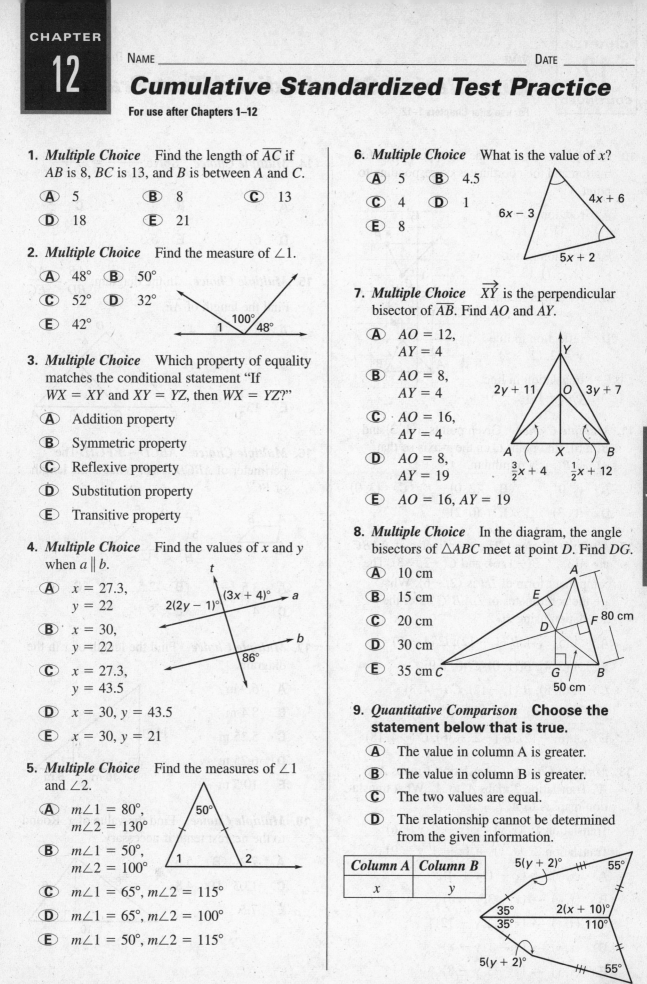

1. Multiple Choice Find the length of $\overline{AC}$ if AB is 8, BC is 13, and B is between A and C.

  Ⓐ 5   Ⓑ 8   Ⓒ 13

  Ⓓ 18   Ⓔ 21

2. Multiple Choice Find the measure of $\angle 1$.

  Ⓐ 48° Ⓑ 50°

  Ⓒ 52° Ⓓ 32°

  Ⓔ 42°

3. Multiple Choice Which property of equality matches the conditional statement "If $WX = XY$ and $XY = YZ$, then $WX = YZ$?"

  Ⓐ Addition property

  Ⓑ Symmetric property

  Ⓒ Reflexive property

  Ⓓ Substitution property

  Ⓔ Transitive property

4. Multiple Choice Find the values of x and y when $a \parallel b$.

  Ⓐ $x = 27.3$, $y = 22$

  Ⓑ $x = 30$, $y = 22$

  Ⓒ $x = 27.3$, $y = 43.5$

  Ⓓ $x = 30$, $y = 43.5$

  Ⓔ $x = 30$, $y = 21$

5. Multiple Choice Find the measures of $\angle 1$ and $\angle 2$.

  Ⓐ $m\angle 1 = 80°$, $m\angle 2 = 130°$

  Ⓑ $m\angle 1 = 50°$, $m\angle 2 = 100°$

  Ⓒ $m\angle 1 = 65°$, $m\angle 2 = 115°$

  Ⓓ $m\angle 1 = 65°$, $m\angle 2 = 100°$

  Ⓔ $m\angle 1 = 50°$, $m\angle 2 = 115°$

6. Multiple Choice What is the value of x?

  Ⓐ 5   Ⓑ 4.5

  Ⓒ 4   Ⓓ 1

  Ⓔ 8

7. Multiple Choice $\overrightarrow{XY}$ is the perpendicular bisector of $\overline{AB}$. Find AO and AY.

  Ⓐ $AO = 12$, $AY = 4$

  Ⓑ $AO = 8$, $AY = 4$

  Ⓒ $AO = 16$, $AY = 4$

  Ⓓ $AO = 8$, $AY = 19$

  Ⓔ $AO = 16$, $AY = 19$

8. Multiple Choice In the diagram, the angle bisectors of $\triangle ABC$ meet at point D. Find DG.

  Ⓐ 10 cm

  Ⓑ 15 cm

  Ⓒ 20 cm

  Ⓓ 30 cm

  Ⓔ 35 cm

9. Quantitative Comparison Choose the statement below that is true.

  Ⓐ The value in column A is greater.

  Ⓑ The value in column B is greater.

  Ⓒ The two values are equal.

  Ⓓ The relationship cannot be determined from the given information.

Column A	Column B
x	y

Chapter 12

10. *Multiple Choice* Name the type of transformation and the coordinates corresponding to point A'.

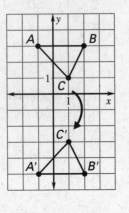

Ⓐ rotation about $(0, 1)$; $(-1, -5)$

Ⓑ rotation about $(1, -1)$; $(3, -5)$

Ⓒ reflection in line $y = -1$; $(-1, -5)$

Ⓓ reflection in line $y = 2$; $(2, -5)$

Ⓔ translation in line $y = -1$; $(2, -5)$

11. *Multiple Choice* Given points $A(1, 2)$ and $B(5, 6)$, find point C on the x-axis so that $AC + BC$ is a minimum.

Ⓐ $\left(\frac{5}{2}, 0\right)$ Ⓑ $(2, 0)$ Ⓒ $(3, 0)$

Ⓓ $(0, 3)$ Ⓔ $(0, 2)$

12. *Multiple Choice* The coordinates of $\triangle ABC$ are $A(3, 2)$, $B(-1, 6)$, and $C(-2, -3)$. The component form of $\overrightarrow{HJ}$ is $\langle 2, -6 \rangle$. What are the coordinates of $\triangle A'B'C'$ after the translation using $\overrightarrow{HJ}$?

Ⓐ $A'(5, -4)$, $B'(1, -12)$, $C'(4, -9)$

Ⓑ $A'(5, 4)$, $B'(1, 0)$, $C'(0, -9)$

Ⓒ $A'(5, 8)$, $B'(1, -12)$, $C'(-4, 3)$

Ⓓ $A'(5, -4)$, $B'(1, 0)$, $C'(0, -9)$

Ⓔ $A'(6, -12)$, $B'(-2, -36)$, $C'(-4, 18)$

13. *Multiple Choice* Translation 1 maps A to A'. Translation 2 maps A' to A''. What translation maps A to A''?

Translation 1: $(x, y) \rightarrow (x - 2, y + 6)$

Translation 2: $(x, y) \rightarrow (x - 1, y - 2)$

Ⓐ $(x, y) \rightarrow (x - 1, y + 4)$

Ⓑ $(x, y) \rightarrow (x - 3, y + 4)$

Ⓒ $(x, y) \rightarrow (x + 2, y - 12)$

Ⓓ $(x, y) \rightarrow (x + 1, y - 8)$

Ⓔ $(x, y) \rightarrow (x - 3, y - 8)$

14. *Multiple Choice* Solve $\dfrac{6}{x + 5} = \dfrac{3}{x - 1}$.

Ⓐ 5   Ⓑ 7   Ⓒ $\dfrac{8}{3}$

Ⓓ 6   Ⓔ 5.3

15. *Multiple Choice* In the diagram, $\dfrac{AB}{BD} = \dfrac{AC}{EC}$. Find the length of $\overline{AE}$.

Ⓐ 8   Ⓑ 4

Ⓒ $5\dfrac{1}{3}$ Ⓓ 12

Ⓔ $13\dfrac{1}{3}$

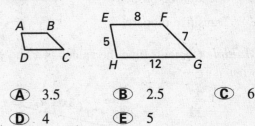

16. *Multiple Choice* $ABCD \sim EFGH$. The perimeter of $ABCD$ is 16. What is the length of $\overline{BC}$?

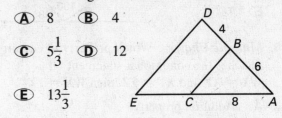

Ⓐ 3.5   Ⓑ 2.5   Ⓒ 6

Ⓓ 4   Ⓔ 5

17. *Multiple Choice* Find the length of x in the diagram.

Ⓐ 6.9 m

Ⓑ 8.4 m

Ⓒ 5.25 m

Ⓓ 6.25 m

Ⓔ 10.5 m

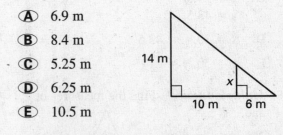

18. *Multiple Choice* Find the value of x. Round to the nearest tenth if necessary.

Ⓐ 7.2   Ⓑ 5.6

Ⓒ 13.3   Ⓓ 4.8

Ⓔ 7.5

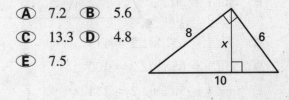

Geometry
Standardized Test Practice Workbook

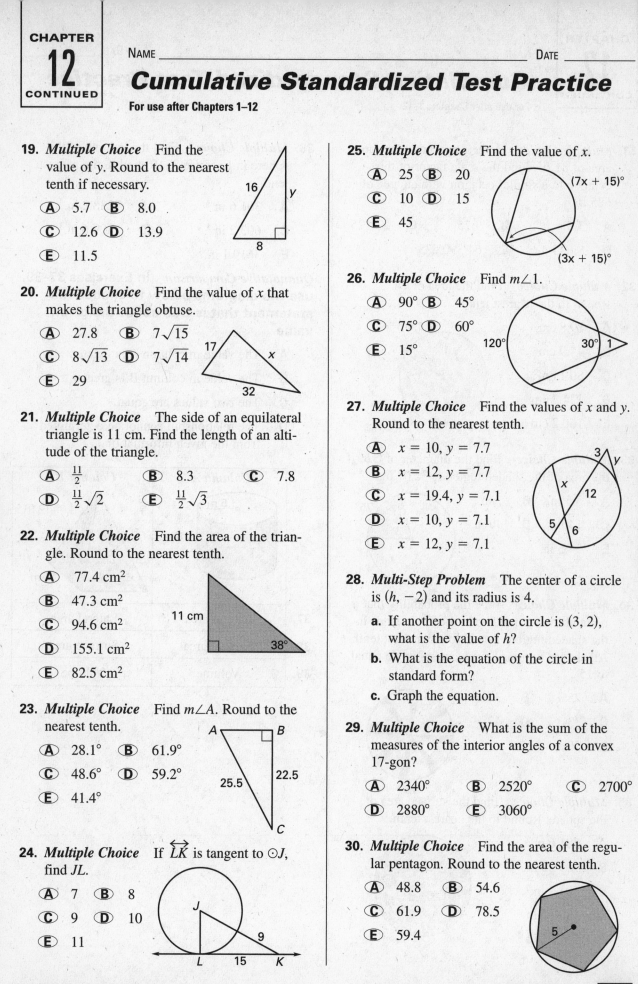

19. *Multiple Choice* Find the value of *y*. Round to the nearest tenth if necessary.

Ⓐ 5.7 Ⓑ 8.0
Ⓒ 12.6 Ⓓ 13.9
Ⓔ 11.5

20. *Multiple Choice* Find the value of *x* that makes the triangle obtuse.

Ⓐ 27.8 Ⓑ $7\sqrt{15}$
Ⓒ $8\sqrt{13}$ Ⓓ $7\sqrt{14}$
Ⓔ 29

21. *Multiple Choice* The side of an equilateral triangle is 11 cm. Find the length of an altitude of the triangle.

Ⓐ $\frac{11}{2}$ Ⓑ 8.3 Ⓒ 7.8
Ⓓ $\frac{11}{2}\sqrt{2}$ Ⓔ $\frac{11}{2}\sqrt{3}$

22. *Multiple Choice* Find the area of the triangle. Round to the nearest tenth.

Ⓐ 77.4 cm²
Ⓑ 47.3 cm²
Ⓒ 94.6 cm²
Ⓓ 155.1 cm²
Ⓔ 82.5 cm²

23. *Multiple Choice* Find *m∠A*. Round to the nearest tenth.

Ⓐ 28.1° Ⓑ 61.9°
Ⓒ 48.6° Ⓓ 59.2°
Ⓔ 41.4°

24. *Multiple Choice* If $\overleftrightarrow{LK}$ is tangent to ⊙*J*, find *JL*.

Ⓐ 7 Ⓑ 8
Ⓒ 9 Ⓓ 10
Ⓔ 11

25. *Multiple Choice* Find the value of *x*.

Ⓐ 25 Ⓑ 20
Ⓒ 10 Ⓓ 15
Ⓔ 45

26. *Multiple Choice* Find *m∠1*.

Ⓐ 90° Ⓑ 45°
Ⓒ 75° Ⓓ 60°
Ⓔ 15°

27. *Multiple Choice* Find the values of *x* and *y*. Round to the nearest tenth.

Ⓐ $x = 10, y = 7.7$
Ⓑ $x = 12, y = 7.7$
Ⓒ $x = 19.4, y = 7.1$
Ⓓ $x = 10, y = 7.1$
Ⓔ $x = 12, y = 7.1$

28. *Multi-Step Problem* The center of a circle is $(h, -2)$ and its radius is 4.

   a. If another point on the circle is $(3, 2)$, what is the value of *h*?

   b. What is the equation of the circle in standard form?

   c. Graph the equation.

29. *Multiple Choice* What is the sum of the measures of the interior angles of a convex 17-gon?

Ⓐ 2340° Ⓑ 2520° Ⓒ 2700°
Ⓓ 2880° Ⓔ 3060°

30. *Multiple Choice* Find the area of the regular pentagon. Round to the nearest tenth.

Ⓐ 48.8 Ⓑ 54.6
Ⓒ 61.9 Ⓓ 78.5
Ⓔ 59.4

Chapter 12

Cumulative Standardized Test Practice

For use after Chapters 1–12

31. *Multiple Choice* A regular octagon has an area of 81 ft². Find the scale factor of this octagon to a similar octagon with an area of 625 ft².

- Ⓐ 3:5
- Ⓑ 9:25
- Ⓒ 27:125
- Ⓓ 8:625
- Ⓔ 64:390,625

32. *Multiple Choice* Find the area of ⊙C. Round to the nearest tenth.

- Ⓐ 89.8 cm²
- Ⓑ 44.9 cm²
- Ⓒ 80.1 cm²
- Ⓓ 134.7 cm²
- Ⓔ 160.2 cm²

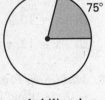

8.1 cm
65°
C

33. *Multiple Choice* Find the diameter of ⊙B, if the area of the shaded region is 32.07 in.².

- Ⓐ 3.5 in.
- Ⓑ 7 in.
- Ⓒ 14 in.
- Ⓓ 49 in.
- Ⓔ 24.5 in.

75°

34. *Multiple Choice* Find the probability that a point chosen at random in the circle lands in the shaded region. Round to the nearest tenth. All shaded regions have a central angle equal to 15°.

- Ⓐ 25%
- Ⓑ 30%
- Ⓒ 33.3%
- Ⓓ 42%
- Ⓔ 50%

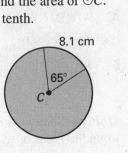

35. *Multiple Choice* Find the surface area of the sphere. Round to the nearest tenth.

- Ⓐ 301.6 in.²
- Ⓑ 7238.2 in.²
- Ⓒ 603.2 in.²
- Ⓓ 1809.6 in.²
- Ⓔ 3619.1 in.²

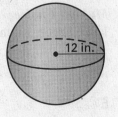

12 in.

36. *Multiple Choice* Find the volume of the sphere in Exercise 35. Round to the nearest tenth.

- Ⓐ 301.6 in.³
- Ⓑ 7238.2 in.³
- Ⓒ 603.2 in.³
- Ⓓ 1809.6 in.³
- Ⓔ 3619.1 in.³

Quantitative Comparison **In Exercises 37–39, use the diagrams below to choose the statement that is true about the given value.**

- Ⓐ The value in column A is greater.
- Ⓑ The value in column B is greater.
- Ⓒ The two values are equal.
- Ⓓ The relationship cannot be determined from the given information.

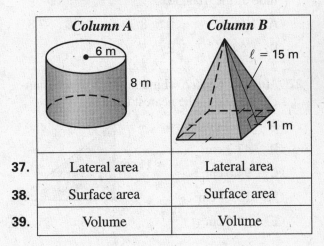

	Column A	Column B
37.	Lateral area	Lateral area
38.	Surface area	Surface area
39.	Volume	Volume

Geometry
Standardized Test Practice Workbook